NORTH AMERICAN
Fighting Uniforms

NORTH AMERICAN
Fighting Uniforms

AN ILLUSTRATED HISTORY SINCE 1756

Edited by Michael Bowers

BLANDFORD PRESS
POOLE · DORSET

First published in the U.K. 1984 by Blandford Press
Link House, West Street, Poole, Dorset BH15 1LL

Copyright © 1984 Blandford Press Ltd

Distributed in the United States by
Sterling Publishing Co., Inc.,
2 Park Avenue, New York N.Y. 10016

British Library Cataloguing in Publication Data

North American fighting uniforms.
  1. United States. *Army*—Uniforms—History
  —Pictorial works
  I. Bowers, Michael
  355.1′4′0973   UC483

ISBN 0 7137 1432 8

Typeset in 8/9pt Rockwell Light by Megaron Typesetting

Printed in Hong Kong by Lee Fung Asco Printers

CONTENTS

Introduction   6

The Seven Years War   7

War of Independence   9

The Birth of the U.S. Cavalry   46

The Civil War   47

Battle of the Little Big Horn   92

World War I   93

World War II   99

Korea   115

Vietnam   116

Special Forces   121

Index   127

INTRODUCTION

This book brings together a fascinating range of North American uniforms – from 1756 to the present day. The illustrations demonstrate the extraordinary influences upon the design of American (and this includes Canadian) uniforms. The Seven Years War of 1756 to 1763 was really a European war fought partly in North America; the War of Independence saw the emergence of a truly American military style. The Civil War, that bitter war between the States, produced many new concepts in uniform design, as well as some fanciful and homespun efforts.

From World War I and World War II, to the elite and special forces in use today, we see in the uniforms a steadily increasing degree of specialisation. The overall picture is one of evolution and adaptation coupled with a rapid development of military sophistication.

THE SEVEN YEARS WAR

Colonel George Washington
In 1754 Washington was given command of the Virginia Militia, a unit in which only the officers appear to have worn uniform, the men wearing their own clothes. During Braddock's expedition the Virginian officers wore buckskin hunting shirts instead of their regimentals, which at that time were blue with scarlet facings and silver lace, scarlet waistcoat, and blue breeches. By 1759 they were wearing blue, with scarlet facings and gold lace, and scarlet waistcoat and breeches.

Private, Quebec Militia
The French colonists of New France constantly allied themselves with the various Indian tribes.
In 1759 the Militia companies were brigaded, each brigade being distinguished by the colour of their knitted woollen cap, or *Tuque*, red for Quebec, white for Trois Rivières, and blue for Montreal. This and the multi-coloured woollen sash worn by this figure were typical items of Canadian folk dress. The Militiaman's equipment consisted of musket, cartouche box, and tomahawk.

Fusilier, Compagnies Franches de la Marine
All the French colonies in America came under the Minister of Marine. By 1757 there were 40 such companies in Canada, mainly stationed in large fortified places, although some also served on the frontiers. The Fusilier shown here wears a *bonnet de police*, regimental waistcoat, and Indian leggings. The regulation coat was grey-white with blue cuffs and lining, sergeants having 2 rows of gold lace round their cuffs. The drummers wore the King's 'small' livery, and the shells of the drums were painted blue.

THE SEVEN YEARS WAR

Private, His Majesty's Independent Companies of American Rangers
'Rangers' were superior Militia raised among trappers and frontiersmen, who were adept in native warfare and woodcraft. The celebrated 'Rogers' Rangers' were formed in 1757 from the 'ranging companies' of the New Hampshire Provincial Regiment, but, although they were paid by the King, they were neither regulars nor provincials. Starting off with a company of 4 officers and 60 men the Rangers gradually increased to battalion strength including a company of Indians led by their own 'officers'. Between 1756 and 1759

Rogers waged constant guerrilla warfare against the French, penetrating enemy territory in the dead of winter, destroying settlements and Indian villages, and watching the progress of the new French Fort Carillon (Ticonderoga). Some of the engagements were extremely bloody affairs, and in the celebrated 'Battle of the Snow-shoes' in the winter of 1758, 146 of Rogers' Rangers were killed. In 1757 Rogers formed a cadet company which trained officers from the regulars in the art of forest-fighting. An attempt was made to keep the clothing in each company uniform, some wearing green and

others grey. The Indians wore their own dress. The Ranger here wears a green hunting shirt, and a Scottish bonnet; and has his snow-shoes slung across his back.

French Colonial Artilleryman
In 1743 an artillery company of *cannoniers-bombardiers* was established at Louisberg, followed by several more companies in Canada in 1750. Twenty officers and men were sent out from France in 1757 to reinforce the Colonial artillerymen. Sergeants wore two stripes of silver lace round their cuffs and corporals 1; the drummers wore the King's 'small' livery.

THE WAR OF INDEPENDENCE

Provincial Alarm Companies and Minutemen

As the disputes with the mother country worsened the colonists began to arm the local militia and form special Alarm Companies of minutemen who could turn out, fully armed and equipped, at a moment's notice. Uniforms do not seem to have been in evidence either at Lexington and Concord or Bunker Hill where, according to Lieutenant Clarke of the marines, both officers and men wore their own clothes, nor did he see 'any colours to their regiments'. What little we know of the dress of the rebel militia suggests that they turned out in much the same way as they would for hunting or shooting, and sporting pictures of the period have suggested the figures shown here.

Naturally with differing drills and weapons, the militia were no match for regular troops in close order but as they showed early on they were not to be despised as skirmishers. As Lord Percy said of them,

Whoever looks upon them merely as an irregular mob will find himself much mistaken; they have men amongst them who know what they are about, having been employed as Rangers against the Canadians and Indians – nor are their men devoid of the spirit of enthusiasm, as we experienced yesterday, for many of them concealed themselves in houses and advanced within ten yards to fire at me and the other officers, though they were morally certain of being put to death themselves in an instant . . .

United States Militiamen
This version of the American
militiaman, with his cap inscribed
'Liberty or Death' – a foretaste of the
French revolution – is based on a
British caricature of the times. He is
armed with a tomahawk, besides his
firearm, and carries his belongings
wrapped in a blanket and worn as a
bandolier.

Officer of Militia
Since officers of the militia were
elected by their companies, they
were often little better than the men
they tried to command, and
generally differed little in
appearance. The officer shown

here, however, is quite smartly
dressed in civilian clothes and
wears a crimson sash round his
waist as a sign of his officer status.
He is armed with a small sword and
half-pike although very often these
were abandoned in favour of fusils
or muskets.

**Private, 4th Connecticut Regiment
of 1775 (Colonel Benjamin Hinman)**
This regiment, one of six raised by
the state of Connecticut, existed
from 1 May to 20 December 1775.
Each was to have ten companies of
100 privates with the usual
complement of officers, N.C.O.s
and drummers. On 14 June 1775

they were taken into Continental
pay until December 1775 when most
of the men returned home on the
expiry of their enlistments. Two
companies of this regiment were
garrisoned at Fort Ticonderoga.
The broad-brimmed hat, the jacket
of nautical cut and the striped
trousers all feature in deserter
descriptions of the time.

THE WAR OF INDEPENDENCE

Private, Pennsylvania Rifle Regiment

Raised in July 1775 from frontiersmen from the western borders of the Province to form a regiment of six companies, each of sixty-eight men, the Pennsylvania Rifle Regiment took part in the siege of Boston. Two companies accompanied Benedict Arnold to Canada and were captured at Quebec. During the winter of 1775–1776 it was reorganised as the 1st Continental Regiment. This figure wears typical Indian dress, in this case (as described in deserter advertisements), dyed black. The hat with a feather or tuft of animal's fur, the fringed rifle frock and the leggings complete an outfit which Washington would have liked to issue to all his army.

Officer, 1st Rhode Island Regiment of 1775 (Varnum)

Under Christopher Greene, cousin of the celebrated Nathanael Greene, the 1st Battalion of this regiment made the heroic march with Arnold to Quebec. Captain Samuel Ward of the regiment is shown in Trumbull's painting of the death of Montgomery at Quebec. The figure here, based upon the painting, shows the type of winter clothing used in the Canadian forests. The pouch and belt are of 'wampum' or Indian beadwork.

Private, Colonel Seth Warner's Battalion of Green Mountain Boys

The disputes between the settlers of the New Hampshire Grants and the New York Colonial officials caused the men of the various towns of New Hampshire and Vermont to form military companies, known as the 'Green Mountain Boys'. In June 1775 Congress formed them into a battalion of 500 men under Seth Warner. The figure here wears the normal uniform of the regiment with the addition of a wampum pouch and belt and a tomahawk.

Private, 4th Independent Maryland State Troops

Seven companies, each of 100 men, were raised in January 1776 to join Washington in New York. The 4th Company was commanded by Captain Hindeman who with a budget of £3 10s per head clothed his men in dyed Osnaberg linen hunting shirts with red collars and cuffs. The state also raised two companies of matrosses and one of marines.

Officer, Colonel Sargent's Massachusetts Battalion

On 19 May 1775, the state of Massachusetts raised twelve battalions of infantry, each of 500 men in ten companies. These battalions were taken into Continental pay on 14 June 1775 and served until the following December. The green coats, and black facings of Colonel Sargent's battalion are mentioned in deserter descriptions. The yellow cockade in the hat donates the rank of field officer.

Private, Colonel Patterson's Massachusetts Battalion

Another of the twelve battalions raised in May 1775, with a similar history to Colonel Sargent's battalion. The blue coats with buff facings are mentioned in deserter descriptions.

THE WAR OF INDEPENDENCE

Gunner, Lamb's New York Artillery Company

The American artillery at Bunker Hill did not distinguish itself. Captain Lamb's company was raised in New York in July 1775 for Continental service. The blue and buff uniform was unusual for artillery units, the majority of whom wore blue, or black, faced with red. The canvas belt over the right shoulder has a drag rope for manhandling the guns attached to it.

Officer, Colonel Knox's Artillery Regiment

Formed over the winter of 1775–1776 from the remnants of Colonel Gridley's regiment and other artillery units in Washington's army, this regiment consisted of twelve companies of five officers, three sergeants, three corporals, one drummer, one fifer, six gunners, six bombardiers, and thirty matrosses. At the end of 1776 most of the men returned to their homes. Colonel Knox was responsible for bringing the British pieces captured at Ticonderoga across country in the face of great difficulties, without which the siege of Boston could not have been pursued. Afterwards he commanded the artillery of the Continental army.

Gunner, Rhode Island Train of Artillery

Captain John Crane's artillery company, one of the few well-trained and equipped militia units when the revolution broke out, joined the New England army before Boston in 1775. After May it appears to have been incorporated into Gridley's Massachusetts Artillery Regiment. An example of the distinctive caps worn by this regiment, belonging to Lieutenant Benjamin Carpenter, was picked up on the battlefield of Long Island, and is now in the Museum of the Fraunces Tavern, New York.

Aide-de-camp to a General Officer

Washington organised the Continental army into divisions and brigades. There was difficulty in recognising superior officers, who had no regulation uniforms. In July 1775 all general officers, their aides and brigade-majors were ordered to wear ribbons of various colours across the breast, under the coat, like the ribbons of orders of chivalry. Aides-de-camp and brigade-majors were to wear a green ribbon. The figure here is shown in the uniform of Lamb's Artillery Company in which he at one time served.

United States Commander-in-Chief

By the order of July, 1775, the commander-in-chief of the Continental army was to be distinguished by a blue ribbon. This portrait of General Washington is based on that painted by Charles Wilson Peale for John Hancock in 1776. The blue and buff uniform which Washington customarily wore later became the regulation dress for the staff of the Continental army. The choice of these colours had political undertones, as they were the 'uniform' of the Whig party in England; their Tory opponents adopted blue coats with red collars and cuffs.

Brigadier-General

The generals of the Continental army were at first hardly distinguishable from their men. General Israel Putnam had on nothing but a sword-belt over his waistcoat. General officers were always being held up by their own sentries, until the order of July 1775, by which they were to wear pink ribbons. Soon major-generals were given purple ribbons. The figure here is based on a popular print of Brigadier-General Benedict Arnold, published in 1776.

THE WAR OF INDEPENDENCE

Rifleman, 1st Continental Regiment
On 1 January 1776, Washington reorganised the Continental army into twenty-seven regiments of infantry. The 1st 'Continental or Foot Regiment in the Service of the United Colonies', and the only one of the twenty-seven to come from Pennsylvania, was formed from Hand's Pennsylvania Rifle Regiment. The regiments continued to wear frontier dress.

Private, 12th Continental Regiment
No less than sixteen of the twenty-seven new Continental regiments of 1776 came from Massachusetts. The 12th, commanded by Colonel

Moses Little, was one of the few regiments properly uniformed in brown with red facings. An order of 4 April 1776, states that,

Col. Hitchcock's and Col. Little's regiments are to turn out tomorrow morning to escort His Excellency into town, to parade at 8 o'clock, both officers and men dressed in uniform, & those of the non-commissioned officers and soldiers that turn out to be washed both face & hands, clean, their beards shaved, their hair combed & powdered, & their arms cleaned . . .

Sergeant, 6th Continental Regiment
The 6th Continental Regiment of 1776, also known as 'Whitcomb's Rangers' after Colonel Asa

Whitcomb, was another Massachusetts regiment which formed part of the Northern army on Lake Champlain. Deserter descriptions of the regiment mention brown coats with red or white facings, and seamen's clothing. Lack of uniform in the Continental army made it difficult to differentiate between officers, N.C.O.s and men. Rank badges had to be adopted which were not only clearly visible, but easily made from materials that were to hand. By an order of July 1775, N.C.O.s were to be distinguished by epaulettes, or strips of cloth, sewed on the right shoulder.

THE WAR OF INDEPENDENCE

Private, 14th Continental Regiment
A provisional regiment of minute-men was raised in Marblehead, Massachusetts, on 14 May 1775 by a prominent ship owner, John Glover. Most of the men were seamen and fishermen and many of them retained their seagoing clothes when the regiment joined the Continental army. On 1 January 1776 the regiment became the 14th Continental Regiment. Descriptions of the dress of the regiment mention 'light coloured coats', drab or brown, with red facings. A well-disciplined regiment, Glover's Marbleheaders achieved immortal fame by being selected to ferry the

army across the frozen Delaware River on Christmas Eve 1776, prior to Washington's surprise attack on Trenton.

Officer, 8th Continental Regiment
Colonel Enoch Poor's 2nd New Hampshire Regiment, formed on 20 May 1775, entered the Continental service in June 1775 and became the 8th Continental Regiment in January 1776. It served with the Northern army until the end of 1776 when its term of service came to an end. Although officers in the Continental army retained crimson sashes and in some cases gorgets typical of the British army, and were

armed with spontoons and fusils, from July 1775 their ranks were distinguished by cockades in the hat. These were red or pink for field officers, yellow for captains (changed in 1776 to white or buff) and green for subalterns.

Private, 18th Continental Regiment
Originally Colonel Phinney's regiment, one of the twelve Massachusetts battalions raised on 19 May 1775. Shortly after entering Boston on 20 March 1776 the 18th Continental were supplied with coats and jackets made of undyed cloth straight off the loom, apparently with buff facings.

THE WAR OF INDEPENDENCE

Private, 2nd New York Regiment, 1775

The state of New York raised four regiments for Continental service in 1775, all of which served with the Northern army. By August 1775 they were all supplied with uniform coats, and according to one witness had acquired 'the air of Regulars'. The 2nd Regiment commanded by Colonel Goose van Schaik wore brown coats faced with blue.

Private, Light Company, 2nd Canadian Regiment

On 10 November 1775, Congress raised a Canadian battalion which was followed in January 1776 by a second battalion. This battalion was recruited 'at large' and was not allocated to any state line, so it was generally known as 'Congress's Own' or 'Hazen's Regiment' after its commander. The regiment was engaged in the retreat across New Jersey in the autumn of 1776, and maintained an exceptionally good record throughout the war in spite of having all foreigners in the army, with the exception of those in Armand's corps, sent to it in 1781. Hazen's Regiment is one of the few that are known to have had a light company as early as 1776. They wore special caps emblazoned with C.O.R., for 'Congress's Own

Regiment', and the motto PRO ARIS ET FOCIS.

Private, 3rd New York Regiment, 1775

The 3rd New York Regiment of 1775 had a similar history to the 2nd Regiment. Commanded by Colonel James Clinton, the regiment wore grey, faced with green.

Private, Delaware Regiment (Haslet's)

Lefferts shows this regiment with leather caps, but recent research has now revealed that the example which he copied is almost certainly a modern reconstruction. In fact, instead of caps there is evidence that the regiment received 'felt hats' in 1776. The style of hat shown here is based on a representation 'of an American soldier' on the Grand Seal of Delaware State.

Officer, 2nd New York Regiment

This regiment was one of four new battalions raised to serve with the Continental army for the year 1776. New York had raised four regiments in 1775 which had served with the Northern army. The four regiments of 1776 served with the main army. The 2nd New York Regiment was commanded by Lieutenant-Colonel Peter Gansevoort from August to November 1776, and the uniform shown in this figure is based on a coat and waistcoat reputed to have been worn by him.

Private, Maryland Regiment (Smallwood's)

This regiment was formed in 1776 from independent companies in Baltimore and Annapolis, one of which, Mordecai Gist's Baltimore Independent Cadets, wore red coats with buff facings. When the regiment joined Washington's army at New York, however, the men were dressed in hunting shirts of various colours. After covering Washington's retreat at the Battle of Long Island, the remains of the regiment were formed during the winter of 1776–1777 into the 1st Maryland Regiment, virtually wiped out at the Battle of Camden.

THE WAR OF INDEPENDENCE

Private, 3rd New York Regiment of 1776
This regiment had a similar history to the 1st New York Regiment and served with the main army until it was disbanded at the end of the year. 'Blue or brown regimentals turned up with green' are mentioned for this regiment in deserter descriptions for 1776.

Officer, 3rd Pennsylvania Battalion of 1776
This battalion raised early in 1776 was reorganised in the winter of 1776–1777 as the 4th Pennsylvania Regiment of 1777. It took part in the New York campaign and surrendered to General Knyphausen after the taking of Fort Washington. The orders regarding rank badges issued in 1775 specified green cockades for subaltern officers. The officer shown here also has a crimson sash, and is armed with a fusil and a bayonet which is suspended from a waist-belt worn over the shoulder. Brown faced with white is mentioned in several deserter descriptions for this regiment in Pennsylvania in the spring of 1776.

Private, 1st Pennsylvania Battalion of 1777
This battalion was created in the winter of 1776–1777 from new recruits and Continental army veterans. 'A regimental brown coat faced with green the buttons marked Pa, Bn, button-holes bound with red', is mentioned in the *Maryland Journal* for 18 February 1777.

Corporal, 6th Virginia Regiment of 1777

Early in 1777, the 6th Virginia was reorganised and served until 14 September 1778, when it was incorporated into the 2nd Virginia Regiment. A deserter of Captain Fox's company of the regiment disappeared, according to the *Pennsylvania Packet* for 13 May 1778, in a 'Light gray coat and waistcoat, the coat faced with green osnabrug overalls, a small round hat with a piece of bearskin in it' This description has formed the basis for this figure, who in addition . has the green shoulder-strap on the right shoulder denoting a corporal.

Private, 9th Pennsylvania Regiment of 1776

Raised in October 1776 as part of an expanded quota from Pennsylvania, this regiment served until January 1781 when it was disbanded on Washington's orders, after the mutiny of the Pennsylvania Line. Deserter descriptions for the regiment in Pennsylvania during the spring of 1777 mention new brown uniform coats, turned up with red, and in one case a light infantry cap is mentioned.

Sergeant, 7th Pennsylvania Regiment of 1777

In the winter of 1776–1777, the former 6th Pennsylvania Battalion was reformed as the 7th Pennsylvania Regiment. Under this title it served until January 1781. The regimentals of the corps appear to have been blue with red facings. The red shoulder-strap denotes a sergeant.

THE WAR OF INDEPENDENCE

Private, Colonel William R. Lee's Additional Continental Regiment
In January 1777 sixteen additional regiments were raised for service with the Continental army. This regiment was formed by William R. Lee mainly from Massachusetts recruits. In April 1779 it was amalgamated with Colonel Jackson's Additional Continental Regiment. According to the *Continental Journal* for 19 December 1777, some of the men wore brown regimental coats faced with red and felt hats.

Private, Colonel Henley's Additional Continental Regiment
Formed in January 1777 by David Henley from Massachusetts recruits, this regiment was amalgamated with Colonel Jackson's Additional Continental Regiment in April 1779. The *Independent Chronicle* for 5 March 1778 mentions a deserter wearing a red coat faced with light blue, and a light infantry cap.

Corporal, Colonel Hartley's Additional Continental Regiment
Formed in January 1777 by Thomas Hartley from Pennsylvania and Maryland recruits. In January 1779 it formed part of the new 11th Pennsylvania Regiment. The *Pennsylvania Gazette* for May 1777 mentions a blue regimental coat with white facings.

Private, Colonel Samuel B. Webb's Additional Continental Regiment

Raised in January 1777 by Samuel B. Webb from Connecticut recruits, this regiment was extremely well-disciplined, trained and dressed. It was always uniformed and even had a band. It was taken into the Connecticut line as the 5th Regiment on 18 July 1780. Between 1778 and 1780 there are several references to the red coats with yellow facings worn by this regiment.

Officer, Colonel Sherburne's Additional Continental Regiment

This was raised in January 1777 by Henry Sherburne from Connecticut and Maryland recruits. On 1 May 1780 it was broken up and many of the men went into Colonel Webb's regiment. Early in 1779, there are several references to deserters in brown coats faced with yellow.

Private, Colonel Spencer's Additional Continental Regiment

Oliver Spencer raised this unit in January 1777 from New Jersey recruits. From 1777 to mid-1778 it was sometimes referred to as the 5th New Jersey Regiment. It was disbanded in January 1781. The *Pennsylvania Packet* for 22 April 1777 refers to a deserter in a 'blue coat with red facings, blanket trousers buttoned down his legs'.

THE WAR OF INDEPENDENCE

Sergeant, 1st Continental Light Dragoons

The American Corps of Light Dragoons dated from the autumn of 1777 when Brigadier-General Count Casimir Pulaski was appointed 'Commander of the Horse' with four weak regiments serving under him. In December 1776 two uniforms seem to have been in use, one blue faced with red and one brown faced with green. Orders issued by Bland in the spring of 1777 give one of the most complete descriptions known of a Continental regiment even to the extent of specifying a comprehensive system of rank markings. Field officers were to have two fringed epaulettes, captains one on the right shoulder, and a gold strap on the left shoulder, and staff officers two plain gold straps. Quartermaster-sergeants had green shoulder-straps, edged with yellow braid and with a green rosette on the right side, sergeants had green shoulder-straps with a green rosette and yellow fringe on the right side, and corporals green shoulder-straps, with a green fringe on the left side. The trumpeters of the regiment wore green faced with brown.

Officer, 3rd Continental Light Dragoons

Raised in January 1777 by George Baylor from Virginians, Pennsylvanians and Marylanders. On 27 September 1778, the regiment was ambushed at Tappan, New York. Only twenty escaped out of 104, Baylor being wounded and captured. Portraits of Captain Roger Nelson, and of Colonel William Washington who commanded the regiment after Baylor's capture, provide evidence for the white uniform with light blue facings.

Private, Light Horse Troop of Philadelphia, 1776–7

From contemporary descriptions and paintings. Members of this exclusive gentlemen's club provided their own uniforms and equipment, including the finest British arms.

Private, Captain Henry Lee's 5th Troop, 1st Continental Light Dragoons, 1776–7

The Virginia State Public Store issued brown coats to this regiment's 1st Troop; and blue coats with red collars and cuffs to the 2nd, 3rd and 4th. Although the record is mute on what uniform the 5th and 6th Troops had, it was probably the coat pictured here. A return of 10 May 1777, revealed that thirty-two spears were distributed to the 1st and 5th Troops.

Private, 1st Continental Light Dragoons, 1777–8

Based on Colonel Theodoric Bland's 'Regimental Order' of 13 April 1777. Interrupted lapels and green hearts on the elbows gave this unit's regimentals a unique appearance. All ranks wore green waistcoats. Hardy leather breeches were favoured by cavalrymen on both sides during the War.

THE WAR OF INDEPENDENCE

Private, 13th Virginia Regiment
Raised in October 1777 as part of Virginia's increased quota, this regiment was in Brigadier-General Peter Muhlenberg's brigade at Valley Forge. The *Pennsylvania Gazette* for 22 April 1778 mentions a blue coat with yellow facings for this regiment. Baron von Steuben noted that at Valley Forge he saw officers whose full uniform at the grand parade consisted of either dressing-gowns or suits made out of blanketing. Officers were permitted to go out to dinner in any clothing they could muster, while the rank and file, going on leave, might spend a day or two making up suits

out of blankets so as to be decently clad on their journey home.

Sergeant, 1st Battalion Philadelphia Associators
The Associators of Philadelphia were companies of volunteer militia of which only two are known to have been active in 1775. Within a few weeks of Lexington, however, these had been increased to four uniformed battalions and several independent companies. In late 1776, or early 1777, they were reorganised as the Philadelphia Brigade under Brigadier-General Cadwalader, and eventually became the 3rd Pennsylvania

Brigade. The uniform of the Associators was brown with different coloured cockades and facings for each battalion.

Private, Light Infantry, 1st Battalion Philadelphia Associators
The light infantry companies attached to the battalions of Associators appear to have been dressed in green with 'smart caps and feathers'.

Lieutenant, 3rd Massachusetts Regiment

This regiment was raised in November 1776 and served until November 1783. The uniform of a Lieutenant Leonard Chapin, stolen from his house according to the *New York Packet* of 21 October 1779, consisted of 'A blue lapelled coat edged with red, Continental buttons, . . . resembling silver, a good silver epaulet, lined with red; the said coat had been turned, and was lined with blue'.

Lieutenant, 8th Massachusetts Regiment

This regiment served from November 1776 to June 1783. A deserting officer, noted in the *Boston Gazette* for 20 December 1777, wore a 'Pale blue uniform coat, faced with red, and a gold epaulet on his right shoulder'.

Sergeant, 14th Massachusetts Regiment

This regiment served from January 1777 to January 1781. The *Independent Chronicle* for 22 October 1778 reported a deserter wearing a 'dark brown regimental coat, faced with light blue, reddish-brown waistcoat, peach blossom trousers'. Blue coats faced with white are also mentioned.

THE WAR OF INDEPENDENCE

Private, 1st Maryland Regiment of 1777

This regiment was formed during the winter of 1776–1777 from a cadre of Smallwood's Maryland Regiment, and suffered severely at the Battle of Camden. Deserters described in the *Maryland Journal* for 9 December 1777 wore blue regimental coats faced with red. One wore a light infantry cap 'with silver lace round the edge, and B.L.I. in cypher in front'. This B.L.I. is thought to have stood for the Baltimore Light Infantry.

Sergeant, 2nd Maryland Regiment of 1777

Formed in December 1776 from the remnants of several Maryland State Independent Companies, this regiment was decimated at Camden. Three deserters from the regiment are recorded in the spring and summer of 1777 as wearing blue coats faced with scarlet.

Corporal, 6th Maryland Regiment of 1777

This regiment was created in December 1776, as part of the Maryland quota, and was virtually destroyed at Camden. Brigadier-General Smallwood formed the remains of the regiments at Camden into an effective regiment in the autumn of 1780, which was divided into two battalions in 1781. Several deserters are recorded in the late summer of 1777 as wearing brown or grey coats turned up with green.

Private, 2nd New Hampshire Regiment

Created, with the 1st New Hampshire Regiment, in the winter of 1776, this regiment served until March 1782, when the New Hampshire line was reorganised. According to Lefferts one company at least wore light blue coats faced with red and lined with white.

Private, 3rd New Jersey Regiment

Recruited in the winter of 1776–1777, this regiment served until broken up in January 1781. According to Lefferts, the coats of the regiment were blue with red facings, and the hats were bound with white or yellow lace, although some leather caps were also worn.

Sergeant, 5th New York Regiment

Raised in the summer of 1776, this regiment served in the Northern Department. In October 1777 most of the regiment was captured at Fort Montgomery. A deserter of the regiment, advertised in the *New York Journal* of 14 July 1777, wore a brown coat faced with blue. Another had a blue coat with button-holes bound with pale blue lace.

THE WAR OF INDEPENDENCE

Private, Butler's Rangers

Major John Butler, an officer of Sir William Johnson's Indian Department, was authorised to raise a corps of eight companies in September 1776. Two of the companies were to be recruited from persons 'speaking the Indian language and acquainted with their customs and manner of making war'. The Rangers were used principally in frontier raids, usually in company with Johnson's, King's Royal Regiment of New York, and Brant's Mohawks. The intention was to arm the corps with rifles but as each man bought his own, a variety of arms was used. The coats of the regiment were green with red facings, no doubt part of the original stock sent out from England.

Loyalist Officer at the Burial of General Fraser

Graham's painting of the burial of General Fraser contains some interesting uniform details. One of the figures, standing in the right foreground and dressed as shown here with the addition of a hat and an Indian belt, appears to be an officer of a Provincial corps. Another officer, probably British, has a short red jacket with dark facings and brown Indian leggings.

Private, Royal Highland Emigrants

This regiment of two battalions, which was taken on the regular establishment in the spring of 1779 as the 84th Regiment, was raised in the autumn of 1775 by Colonel Allan Maclean from the families of men of the 42nd, 77th and 78th Highlanders, who had settled in Canada at the end of the Seven Years War. Recruits were also obtained from Scottish emigrants in New York and North Carolina. The uniform, facings and tartan of the 84th were the same as the 42nd, and one of the von Germann drawings shows the plaid still in use.

Private, Pennsylvania State Regiment, 1777

The so-called 'State Troops' were those who were neither in Continental service, nor militia. Early in 1777 Pennsylvania had a State artillery regiment, which was taken into Continental service in July 1777, and an infantry regiment, which was taken into Continental service in November of the same year. Three Pennsylvania newspapers around the date of 20 August 1777 report four deserters 'all dressed in blue, turned up with red, and white pewter buttons with the letters P.S.R. marked on them'.

Private, 5th Pennsylvania Regiment, 1777

The 5th Pennsylvania Regiment was formed in January 1777 around a nucleus of Anthony Wayne's 4th regiment. The 5th was one of the two regiments (the 9th was the other) which did not immediately join in the mutiny of the Pennsylvania line in 1781. The 5th retained their original blue coats with white facings until 1778 when the supply of white cloth ran out and red was used instead. From documents relating to the 2nd Pennsylvania Regiment it appears that in some cases whole regiments, and not just

the light companies, wore caps. The curious red flannel leggings are mentioned in connection with Wayne's Brigade in early 1779.

Private, 11th Pennsylvania Regiment, 1777

The 11th Regiment was formed in October 1776 and served until its merger with the 10th Regiment in July 1778. The *Pennsylvania Evening Post* of 22 April 1777 mentions a 'new suit of regimentals, consisting of a light infantry cap, blue coat with scarlet cape and cuffs, white woollen waistcoat, new buckskin breeches'.

THE WAR OF INDEPENDENCE

'American Officer', 1778
This figure, after a drawing by von Germann, shows an officer of an unidentified Continental regiment in 1778. On 1 January 1778 Washington ordered 'New Cloathing' for the Continental army, which he described in a letter as 'a garment of the pattern of the Sailor's sea Jacket' which '. . . sets close to the body and by buttoning over the breast, adds much to the warmth of the Soldier'. There could, he added, be 'a small cape and cuff of a different colour to distinguish the Corps'.

Officer, 5th Virginia Regiment, 1777
The 5th Virginia Regiment was reorganised early in 1777 and commanded by Josiah Parker from April 1777 to July 1778. A miniature of Colonel Parker by Charles Willson Peale, part of the National Collection of Fine Arts, Washington, D.C., shows him in a typical Virginian uniform of blue, faced in red, with the addition of narrow gold lace on the button-holes.

'American Soldier', 1778
Another von Germann drawing shows a private of an unidentified American regiment, with the unusual combination of a grey jacket with yellow facings.

THE WAR OF INDEPENDENCE

Soldier in Canadian Winter clothing, 1778
This figure is based on von Germann's drawing titled 'Ein Canadischer Bauer', which shows the typical winter dress of the inhabitants of Canada, which was adopted by the participants on both sides.

Officer, Continental Regiment of Artillery Artificers
In January 1777, Benjamin Flower, Commissary of Military Stores, raised several units of 'artificers' which fulfilled the rôle of the modern Ordnance Corps, supervising the manufacture and maintenance of weapons and transport. This drawing is based on a portrait of Flower attributed to James Peale, brother of Charles Willson Peale.

Officer, Morgan's Rifle Corps, 1777
In the summer of 1777 Washington formed a corps of 500 riflemen, selected from the Main army, which he placed under the command of Colonel Daniel Morgan. The corps joined the Northern army in September 1777, and served with distinction in the Saratoga campaign. After rejoining the Main army in the winter of 1777–1778 the Corps was disbanded. This portrait of Morgan wearing a rifle frock and overalls, with an officer's sash and sword, is based on the figure in Trumbull's painting of the surrender of Burgoyne at Saratoga.

THE WAR OF INDEPENDENCE

Red Jacket

Red Jacket (1751?–1830) was a celebrated orator and chief of the Seneca, one of the Six Nations of the Iroquois, and one of those who supported the British in the American revolution. The Iroquois dress of the period was usually made of red or blue traders' broadcloth, decorated with beads and quills. In this drawing, based on a print slightly later than the revolution, Red Jacket wears a blue cloth hunting shirt, red cloth leggings and deerskin moccasins. He wears a British officers' gorget and crimson sash, and is armed with a musket.

Joseph Brant (Thyandanega)

Joseph Brant, a Mohawk, was supposed to have been the brother of Sir William Johnson's Indian wife. In any case he was brought up by Sir William, and educated at the school of one Dr Wheelock. Afterwards he was employed as an under-secretary at Johnson Hall. After deciding to throw in his lot with the British, Joseph Brant, along with Sir John Johnson and John Butler, was a prominent leader of the raids that ravaged the New York backcountry. After the war Brant led his people to Canada where they settled along the banks of the Great River, in what is now Ontario.

Iroquois Warrior

Until they were supplied with firearms, the Iroquois were mainly armed with the war club, the tomahawk, the bow, and occasionally with a short lance and a shield. As well as these weapons every brave carried a scalping knife. In the early colonial period vigorous attempts were made to prevent the Indians obtaining firearms, but by various means, both legal and illegal, they managed to acquire them. The firearm soon became an object of status, and Indians were prepared to pay vast sums for a weapon, whether it was in firing order or not.

Midshipman, Continental Navy

On 5 September 1776 the Marine Committee of Congress issued the first dress regulations for the United States navy. These provided for a blue coat, with a standing collar, red lapels and cuffs, flat yellow metal buttons, a red waistcoat and blue breeches, as the basic dress. Captains had gold lace on their waistcoats and cuff flaps, while those of lieutenants were plain. Midshipmen had pale blue lapels to their coats.

Captain Abraham Whipple, Continental Navy

Abraham Whipple of Providence, Rhode Island, who was reputed to have fired the first shot of the revolution at sea, took part in the 1772 incident when a royal revenue cutter, the *Gaspée*, ran aground off Narragansett and was burned by the local citizenry. Later he became a noted frigate captain in the Continental navy. With the exception of the cuff flaps, Whipple's dress in this portrait is remarkably like the regulations. In March 1777 a meeting of senior officers proposed a new uniform consisting of a blue coat, lined in white and laced with gold, with gold epaulettes, which was worn by some officers but never officially recognised. In February 1781 Congress issued an order which expressly forbade officers to wear 'any gold lace, embroidery or vellum, other than such as Congress or the Commander-in-chief of the Army or Navy shall direct . . .'

Seaman, Continental Navy

There were no regulations for the dress of the seamen in the Continental navy, and their appearance was much the same as the sailors of the Royal Navy. The sailor here wears a round hat, short jacket and striped trousers, and is armed with a brace of pistols tucked into his belt.

THE WAR OF INDEPENDENCE

Private, Pennsylvania State Marines; Officer, Maryland State Marines
In addition to the Continental, or 'Regular', marines, there were also marines in the navies maintained by several of the states.

Two examples of these marines, a private from Pennsylvania and a Maryland officer are shown here.

Continental Marines, 1776
The first recruiting centre for the Continental marines was the Tun Tavern in Philadelphia, the landlord of which, Captain Mullen, was commissioned in the marines in June 1776. Although he apparently never served at sea, he and his company saw action in the Trenton-Princeton campaign. In September 1776 the Marine Committee of Congress approved a green coat, faced in white, with a silver epaulette on the right shoulder for officers of marines. Probably because of the shortage of white material in Pennsylvania (the depot of the marines remained at Philadelphia),

the facings were changed to red in 1779. The marines were disbanded at the end of the war and were not reformed until 1790.

Aide-de-Camp to a General Officer, 1780

The distinction of rank by sashes and cockades lasted until June 1780. Officers, other than General officers, were to wear the uniforms of their corps. Colonels, lieutenant-colonels and majors were to wear two epaulettes, captains one on the right shoulder, and subalterns one on the left. Aides-de-camp wore the uniform of their regiments, unless they were unattached in which case they wore the uniform of their general, with a green feather in the hat. Aides-de-camp to the commander-in-chief wore green and white feathers.

Major-General the Marquis of Lafayette

By the orders of June 1780, general officers were to wear blue coats with yellow buttons, lined and faced in buff, with two epaulettes and white or buff 'under-cloaths'. Major-generals were to be distinguished by two silver stars on the epaulette strap, and a black and white feather in the hat.

Brigadier-General Anthony Wayne

By the order of June, 1780, brigadier-generals were to be distinguished by one silver star on their epaulette straps, and by a white feather in the hat. The

commander-in-chief seems to have worn three stars on his epaulettes and a plain hat without any feather. The adjutant-general and his assistants were to wear red and green hat feathers. The stars on the epaulettes, in particular, were the same as those used by the corresponding grades of French general officer. The black cockade with a white centre was adopted as a reciprocal gesture to the French who, on their arrival at Newport in July 1780, had paid the compliment of mounting a black American cockade over the white cockade of the Bourbons.

THE WAR OF INDEPENDENCE

Continental Army Regulations of 1779

In September 1778, some 20,000 suits of brown and blue uniforms, faced with red, had been received from France, and with this supply Washington managed to clothe his army for the winter of 1778–1779. In January 1779, Washington submitted to Congress a plan for clothing the army which proposed a different colour for each State with individual regiments of the State Line distinguished by various colours and arrangements of facings, rather in the French style.

In May, the Board of War replied with a plan of their own. It differed in suggesting that all the uniforms (except for those of the waggoners, who were to have brown or grey coats) should be dark blue with white linings and buttons, to be worn with white waistcoats and breeches.

Although Washington approved the plan, and the regulations remained in force until December 1782, it is not clear to what extent the Continental Army actually wore these new uniforms.

Fifer, New Jersey Regiments

Drummers and fifers were ordered to wear the reversed colours of their groups. Those of the fourth, or southern group, wore blue coats with white lacing.

Sergeant, New York Regiments

Sergeants of infantry were to wear silk epaulettes, white for all regiments except those with buff facings, who were to have buff epaulettes.

Field Officer, New Hampshire Regiments

This officer wears the uniform of the Continental Army in accordance to 1779 regulations.

Sergeant, Corps of Continental Artillery

Knox's Brigade of Artillery, which served with the Main army from 1777–1783, consisted of four battalions of twelve companies each, totalling 729 in all ranks. It also had a company of the Regiment of Artillery Artificers, and civilian drivers, attached to it. In 1781 the establishment was changed to nine companies per battalion, totalling 651 all ranks. The uniform shown here is that laid down in the 1779 regulations. Sergeants were to have two yellow silk epaulettes, and corporals two yellow worsted epaulettes.

Officer, Corps of Engineers

There were very few qualified engineers in the Continental army, and most of these were volunteers from the French army. In June 1778 the Corps of Sappers and Miners was formed, to assist the engineers, consisting of three companies of four officers and sixty rank and file, mainly drawn from the ranks of the Connecticut and Massachusetts infantry regiments. By the Order of June 1780, officers of the Corps of Engineers and of the Corps of Sappers and Miners were to wear blue coats, with buff facings and red linings, buff waistcoats and breeches, gold buttons and gold epaulettes of their respective ranks.

Drummer, Corps of Continental Artillery

There was one drummer to each company in each battalion of artillery. They wore uniforms of the reversed colours of the corps.

THE WAR OF INDEPENDENCE

Dragoon, 4th Continental Light Dragoons

Originally dressed in red, this regiment was supplied with captured British coats of the 8th and 24th regiments, but deserter descriptions for the period 1780–1782 mention uniform coats of green, faced red. Sent south in 1780 the regiment suffered badly at Camden, after which the rank and file were taken into Colonel Washington's mixed force. In 1781, it was renamed the 4th Legionary Corps, with an establishment of four mounted and two dismounted troops, totalling 455 of all ranks, and was assigned to the Pennsylvania quota. The figure shown here is dressed for dismounted service.

Officer, 2nd Continental Light Dragoons

According to the Board of War's plan of June 1779, the Continental Light Dragoons were to have blue coats faced with white. The N.C.O.s, farriers and saddlers were to have blue epaulettes, and blue cloaks with white collars and green stable-jackets were also mentioned. The trumpeters were at first supposed to wear the same as the dragoons, but they were later ordered to wear white faced and lined in blue. In January 1781 the regiment was renamed the 2nd Legionary Corps and was assigned to the Connecticut quota. One of the last regiments to serve in the war, some of its men feature in Trumbull's paintings wearing blue faced with buff, and carrying helmets with light blue turbans and yellow tassels. The metal helmet shown here is of a typically French design.

Lieutenant-Colonel Banastre Tarleton, British Legion

Formed by Lord Cathcart in 1778 from loyalists of New York, Pennsylvania and New Jersey, the British Legion achieved considerable notoriety. The figure here is based on the celebrated portrait by Sir Joshua Reynolds in the National Gallery, London, confirmed by a portrait of Colonel George Hanger, who also served in the British Legion. The type of head-dress, which was worn by British light dragoons until 1814, was known as a 'Tarleton' helmet even by the French, suggesting that he was its inventor. An M.S. Almanack

for the year 1783 compiled by a Hessian officer, Bernhard de Wiederhold, and belonging to the New York Historical Society, describes the uniform of the Legion cavalry as 'Short Round Tight Jacketts, Black Collar and Cuffs', and that of the infantry as a 'Short Coat-Green with same lappel, variety button hole (viz. laced) & Black Cuff & Collar'; mounted figures in the background of Tarleton's portrait show the men's jackets as being similar to the officers', but with white lace. There are, however, indications that the British Legion may have worn white while campaigning in the south.

Hussar, Queen's Rangers

In January 1778, a troop of thirty cavalrymen was added to the Queen's Rangers, and shortly after was dressed as hussars. In 1780, three troops of light dragoons were added who, according to Lefferts, wore Tarleton helmets, green jackets, buckskin breeches, and boots, altogether very similar in appearance to the British Legion. The figure here, showing a hussar of the Queen's Rangers in 1780, is based on a set of drawings in the Toronto Central Library made by the Adjutant of the corps, Captain James Murray.

THE WAR OF INDEPENDENCE

Private, 1st Continental Light Dragoons, 1781
Uniform and horse equipment based on a watercolour from the journal of Sub-lieutenant Jean-Baptiste-Antoine de Verger, an officer of the French Royal Deux-Ponts Regiment, who served at Yorktown. This is the uniform Washington prescribed for all his light dragoons in the General Order of 2 October 1779.

Private, Corps of Virginia Light Horse, 1781
A Virginia physician wrote of this motley outfit in his diary: 'Most of our Horse are Volunteers, in small bodies, & chiefly Gentlemen; most of them exceedingly well mounted, but some of them badly armed, & all under very little discipline, & hard to govern.' White canvas stable jackets and coveralls, as well as accoutrements intended for the 3rd Continental Light Dragoons, were issued from Virginia state stores. This fellow wears a simple jockey cap, a hunting sword and carries an aged firelock.

Private, 2nd Continental Light Dragoons, 1781
From another sketch in the Verger journal. Like the other mounted private, this man is armed with Model 1763–66 French carbines and American made broadswords.

Private, Pulaski's Legion Infantry
In March 1778, Count Pulaski was authorised to raise an independent corps consisting of three troops of cavalry, a company of *chasseurs*, one of grenadiers, two of infantry, and a 'supernumary company', totalling some 268 men. In February 1779 Pulaski's Legion was sent south but was disbanded after Pulaski's death before Savannah in October. Clothing returns for the years 1778–1780 reveal that both the cavalry and infantry of the Legion were issued with cavalry-type helmets and blue coats faced with red. The cavalry, however, seem to have worn more conventional jackets or sleeved waistcoats, buckskin breeches and boots.

Brigadier-General Charles Tuffin Armand, Marquis de la Rouerie
Armand, an officer of the French army, took over Baron Ottendorf's Independent Company in June 1777, but it was not until a year later that Armand's 'Free and Independent Chasseurs' were given an establishment of three companies of 150 men each. By August of the same year, however, it had only 153 men in all, many of them former Brunswick prisoners. Charles Willson Peale's portrait of Armand, on which the figure here is based, shows him wearing the single star of a brigadier-general on the straps of his epaulettes, and the cross of the French Order of St Louis.

Trooper, von Heer's Provost Corps
In May and June 1778, a Provost Corps of sixty-three Light dragoons (including four executioners) under the command of Major von Heer, was formed to maintain order in the rear of the Main army. Two N.C.O.s and eight troopers were retained by Washington to carry his despatches until 1783, and were thus the last mounted troops of the Continental army.

Private, 3rd North Carolina Regiment, 1778
Raised in April 1776, this regiment served with the Main army until 1779, when it was reorganised and sent south. Little is known about its uniform, but Lefferts shows men of the regiment in hunting shirts and overalls.

Officer, 1st South Carolina Regiment;
Private, 2nd South Carolina Regiment
The 1st and 2nd South Carolina Regiment, together with a regiment of rangers, were raised in June 1775 for service within the state, but were taken into Continental service. They distinguished themselves in the defence of Fort Moultrie on Sullivan Island during the abortive British attack on Charleston. Both regiments were dressed in blue, sometimes described as black, with red facings, and wore the curious cap with a silver crescent badge associated with South Carolina. That of the 1st Regiment bore the Legend ULTIMA RATIO, and that of the 2nd, LIBERTY, or, LIBERTY OR DEATH. A portrait of Colonel Cotesworth Pinckney shows him in this uniform but with a grenadier cap, which is unfortunately not clear enough to

reproduce here. A list of rebel forces at Charleston published in the *Pennsylvania Ledger* on 28 April 1778 mentions the '1st Regiment Colonel Coteswoth Pinckney 450 men black dress faced red, chiefly Carolinians', and the '2nd Regiment Colonel Huger, 395, same dress and some white frocks, chiefly old countrymen'. Both regiments were captured at the fall of Charleston in 1780.

Private, North Carolina Volunteers
Apart from the fact that 114 men of this regiment were part of Cornwallis's force at Yorktown, little is known about its history. The uniform shown here, red with plain blue lapels, is based on Wiederhold's list.

Lieutenant John Caldwell, British 8th (or the King's) Regiment, in Indian Dress
From 1768 to 1785 the 8th Regiment served in Canada, garrisoning the forts along the St Lawrence and Great Lakes, and taking part in the fierce backcountry fighting. In the painting, from which this figure is taken, Caldwell is shown in the Indian dress that he wore while taking a leading part in the Council held at Wakitomiky on 17 January 1780. He is holding in his hand the wampum belt or 'Hatchet' bearing the design of a tomahawk, which the Americans had sent to the Indians to win over their support.

Sergeant, 3rd Battalion, De Lancey's Brigade
Raised in 1776 among the loyalists of New York State by Oliver De Lancey, this regiment or 'brigade', consisted of three battalions. At first they were dressed in green, but when the Provincial line went into red De Lancey's were given blue facings, with white buttons and lace, arranged in one's, two's or three's according to the battalion. They appear to have worn caps and woollen overalls, red, blue, or brown, in winter and hats in summer. The wide-brimmed white hat shown here appears in American deserter descriptions.

THE WAR OF INDEPENDENCE

Private, Rhode Island Light Infantry Company

The negro soldier, of what seems to be a Rhode Island company (to judge by the shape of the cap and the badge of an anchor on its front), is based on a sketch by Baron von Clausen, one of Rochambeau's aides-de-camp.

Officer, New York Light Infantry Company

According to the Frenchman Chastellux, the officers of the Corps of Light Infantry carried swords and spontoons, and the subalterns fusils and bayonets. The figure here is based on one appearing in Trumbull's painting of the British surrender at Yorktown. He wears a normal New York officer's uniform, with a light infantry cap, and wings under his epaulettes.

Private, Massachusetts Light Infantry Company

Deborah Sampson, a Massachusetts girl, joined the 4th Massachusetts at West Point, posing as a man, and was posted to the light infantry company. The description of her uniform in her biography refers to 'white wings' on the shoulders, and 'cords on the arms and pockets'. The figure here is a reconstruction from this description, with the addition of a light infantry cap of the type shown by Trumbull.

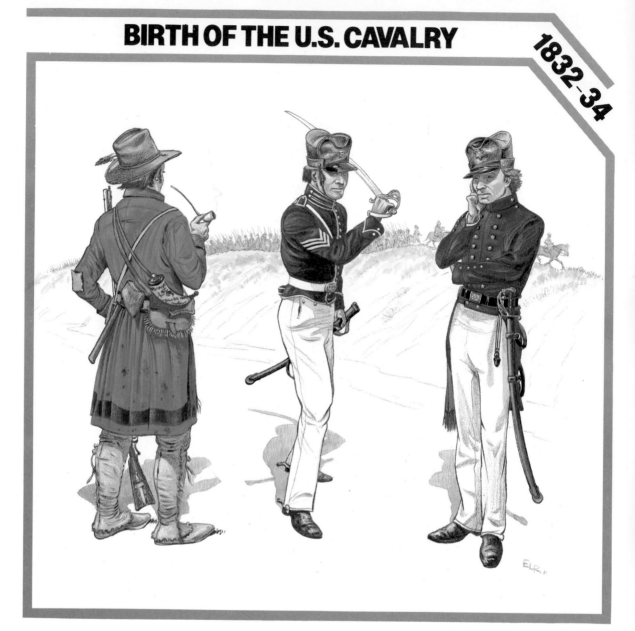

Private, U.S. Mounted Ranger Battalion, 1832
Frontiersmen who provided their own arms, clothing, horses and equipment, the Mounted Rangers were a seedy bunch. Dirty leather hunting shirts, blanket coats and greasy leather leggings were the norm.

Sergeant ('Long Ned'), U.S. Regiment of Dragoons, Fatigue Order, 1833
Many shortages plagued the Regiment of Dragoons as its first battalion was mustered in the summer of 1833. Private James Hildreth said that Captain Edwin V. Sumner's Company B received Model 1833 shell jackets and white cotton pantaloons for drill and fatigue.

Adjutant (Second Lieutenant Jefferson Davis), U.S. Regiment of Dragoons, Undress, 1833
A veteran dragoon remembered seeing the future Confederate President on the parade ground at Jefferson Barracks in 'white drill Pants, made quite narrow at the boot, and quite wide at the thigh, and undress coat.' The officer's collapsible leather forage cap was marked by a gilt, embroidered, six-pointed star. An enlisted man's bore his company's letter cast in brass.

Major-General, Full Dress

In full dress, General Officers wore the regulation double-breasted frock-coat, with collar and cuffs of black or very dark blue velvet. Rank was denoted by the arrangement of the buttons: Brigadier-Generals had buttons in groups of two, eight per row; Major-Generals in threes, nine in each row; and Lieutenant-Generals in fives, ten in each row. Rank was also indicated by the badge on the gold lace epaulettes – one silver star for Brigadier Generals, two for Major Generals, and three for Lieutenant-Generals. The badge on the felt hat consisted of the letters 'U.S.' in silver

embroidery, surrounded by a gold-embroidered laurel wreath; as an alternative to the felt hat, General Officers were authorised to wear a low-crowned black bicorn in full dress, with gold lace decoration; in practice it seems to have been used only rarely. In design it resembled that worn by the Confederate army (illustrated on page 70).

The buff silk waist-sash was a further distinction of rank, as was the ornate shabraque, bearing rank insignia in the form of stars in the rear corners. Laced holster-caps to match the shabraque were sometimes used, though many preferred plain black leather

designs. Swords were carried by all General Officers in full dress; the regulation pattern (Model 1860) had a thin, light blade, often replaced by a more sturdy version for active service.

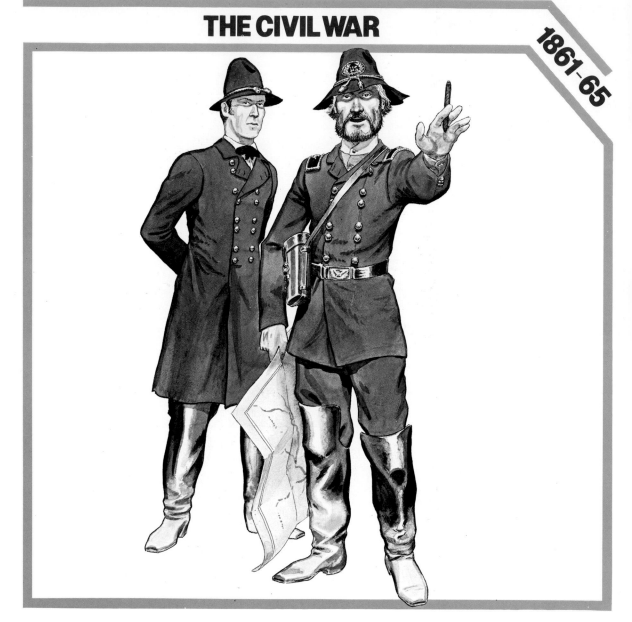

Brigadier-Generals, Service Dress
Both figures on this plate are taken from original photographs, and show how the personal whim of individual officers led to numerous non-regulation styles being worn on active service. The black felt hat could be 'punched up' in the crown to resemble a dunce's cap, which style, though appearing slightly ridiculous, was favoured by General Burnside and extensively copied by his staff. The more usual method of wearing the hat (as shown on the other figure) resembled the full dress style. General McDowell wore a pith helmet as a protection from the sun; it was described as

'like an inverted washbowl'.

Regulation undress uniform consisted of a plain dark blue frock-coat, double-breasted with buttons arranged according to rank as in full dress, with a standing collar, and plain dark blue trousers. In this plate are illustrated two versions, one longer and one shorter than the regulation, both with turned-down collars and one with cut lapels, both revealing the shirt-collar. This type of garment was often worn without rank-bars; indeed, even Ulysses Grant was described on various occasions as being almost indistinguishable from a Union private or even a civilian! Just

before Antietam, Burnside was thus described:

'dressed so as to be almost unrecognizable as a general officer; wore a rough blouse on the collar of which a close look revealed two much-battered and faded stars, indicating his rank . . . he wore a black 'Slouch' hat, the brim well down over his face.'

1st Lieutenant, Cavalry Service Dress; Private, Cavalry Service Dress; Corporal, 2nd Cavalry, Full Dress, 1860–61

When the U.S. Cavalry was reorganised in 1861, the two dragoon regiments became the 1st and 2nd Cavalry.

The black felt hat, standard issue for all branches of the army in full dress, was known as the 'Hardee', 'Kossuth' or 'Jeff Davis' pattern; it had a yellow hatcord and black plume, the latter reserved for parade. On the front was a brass crossed sabres badge with regimental number and company identification letter; the turned-up brim was secured by a brass badge consisting of the U.S. eagle and shield device.

In full dress, the regulation shell-jacket with yellow piping was worn, with two loops of lace at either side of the collar. One such loop was the official distinction of volunteer regiments, but it appears that the 2nd Cavalry (though a regular regiment) also wore one lace. The shoulder-scales and white gloves were reserved for parade. The official Regulations specified dark blue trousers for all branches of the army except Light Artillery, but General Orders of 16 December 1861 authorised the more familiar sky-blue trousers. Equipment was black leather with brass fittings; the Model 1860 light cavalry sabre was the regulation arm, but some units retained the Model 1840 Dragoon sabre.

The most common uniform worn on campaign consisted of the cloth képi and standard pattern fatigue-blouse, occasionally worn with yellow braid trimming. The light blue trousers could be worn either inside or outside the boots. The crossed sabres badge officially worn on the front of the képi was often transferred to the top, to allow the cap to be worn in the fashionable 'pressed-down' style.

THE CIVIL WAR

1st Sergeant, Cavalry, with Sheridan's Guidon; Captain, Cavalry, Full Dress

Cavalry officer's full dress uniform included the 'Hardee' hat with two feather plumes and cords of mixed black and gold. The hat-badge was embroidered in gold on a black velvet oval, consisting of crossed sabres, with regimental number and company letter for company officers up to and including the rank of Captain, and just the regimental number for Majors and upwards.

In full dress, all officers wore the frock-coat, single-breasted with nine buttons for company officers, and double-breasted with two rows of seven buttons for regimental officers. The epaulettes worn in full dress were of gold lace with bullion fringes for all except 2nd Lieutenants, whose epaulettes had thin cord fringes. On the epaulette-strap was a silver circle bearing the regimental number (nearest the 'crescent'), and higher up the badges of rank corresponding to those worn on the shoulder-bars of ordinary dress. Trousers were sky blue (though dark blue was the original regulation), with an ⅛th-inch welt on the outer seam.

The 1st Sergeant illustrated wears a more or less standard campaign dress (the waistbelt being worn under the fatigue jacket); he carries the personal flag of Major-General Philip H. Sheridan, Cavalry Corps, Army of the Potomac (1865) who, like other cavalry leaders, signified his position in the field by his own unique guidon.

Federal cavalry formations did not possess Corps badges as did their infantry counterparts, but two corps had similar badges, worn on the hat or képi. Sheridan's Cavalry corps had a badge consisting of a white sunburst (this badge can be seen on the front of the 1st Sergeant's képi). Wilson's Cavalry Corps had a badge consisting of a horizontal yellow carbine.

1861-65

Sergeant, Cavalry with Custer's Guidon; Officer, 1st Rhode Island Cavalry

The Sergeant wears the regulation full dress shell-jacket, often worn on campaign with the képi. The trousers had 1½-inch yellow stripes on the outer seams for sergeants. The flag carried is typical of the type carried by orderlies of noted cavalry generals, intended to mark their position on the battlefield: Federal generals Sheridan, Kilpatrick, Merritt and Custer all had 'personal' standards or guidons, that illustrated being the third pattern used by General G. A. Custer. Custer's first flag was a red

over blue guidon bearing a crossed sabres badge and two battle honours, the second a more elaborate version with fringe and additional honours, the third that illustrated (bearing the crossed sabres badge in white), and the fourth and final pattern a larger version of the third with a white tape edge.

The figure of the officer of the 1st Rhode Island Cavalry is taken from a photograph of Colonel Alfred Nattie Duffié. Unusual features included in the uniform are the double-breasted shell jacket with yellow piping and very 'full' sleeves, and the 'baggy' trousers,

the whole ensemble appearing much more French than American. That is hardly surprising, as Duffié was a graduate of the St Cyr military academy and fought with great distinction with the French cavalry in Algiers, Senegal and the Crimea. He further distinguished himself when he emigrated to the United States, rising from his commission as Captain in the 2nd New York Cavalry, to command the 1st Rhode Island Cavalry, to Brigadier-General and divisional commander, becoming an outstanding cavalry commander in the Union army.

**Private, Cavalry, in 'gum blanket';
Corporal, Cavalry, with Regimental
Standard**

The sky blue cavalry overcoat was
double-breasted, with a 'stand-and-
fall' collar; the cape, lined yellow,
could be thrown back over the
shoulder. When worn buttoned, the
cape extended to the cuff of the
greatcoat.

Each cavalry regiment carried a
Regimental Standard, similar in
design to the infantry version but
only two feet five inches long by two
feet three inches on the pole. The
blue ground of the standard bore
the design of an eagle with wings
outspread, with a red, white and
blue U.S. shield on its breast, holding
a branch of laurel and a sheaf of
arrows in its talons; above the eagle
was a scroll inscribed 'E PLURIBUS
UNUM' in black lettering, and below
a similar scroll bearing the title of
the regiment. The standard-bearer
illustrated wears the black leather
standard-belt over the coat, but
under the cape, as was usual for all
equipment.

The waterproof 'gum blanket' as
shown on the other figure could
serve as a 'poncho'-style garment,
or (by means of eyelet holes in the
corners) be rigged as a one-man
'pup' tent. One of the most useful
pieces of equipment issued during
the war, it was carried rolled
around the blanket or strapped onto
the knapsack.

Corporal, Cavalry, with Company Guidon; Private, Cavalry, with Designating Flag, Cavalry Reserve Headquarters, Army of the Potomac, 1862

Both figures in this plate are shown in campaign dress, being the basic regulation fatigue dress, but with a number of less official details: the corporal, for example, wears the collar of the fatigue-blouse turned down with a coloured neckerchief under the collar, and the common 'slouch' hat.

Each Federal Corps, Division and Brigade had its own 'Designating Flag' intended to mark the position of the headquarters of the formation at all times. Designating flags were made in a variety of sizes and an even larger variety of designs. That illustrated is the Designating Flag of the Cavalry Reserve Headquarters, Army of the Potomac, which was authorised by a General Order of March 1862. The two brigades of the Cavalry Reserve were assigned flags at the same time, these also being yellow, with a five-pointed blue star in the centre for the 1st Brigade, and two similar stars on the flag of the 2nd.

The corporal is shown carrying a Company Guidon of the pattern used until 1863 and after 1865, consisting of a swallow-tailed flag, the red top bearing the white letters 'U.S.' and the white lower portion the company identifying letter. The flag was flown from a nine-feet long pole, topped by the standard brass heart-shaped pike-head. Between 1863 and 1865 a different pattern of guidon was carried by cavalry companies, of the same shape but consisting of a 'stars and stripes' design like that of the National Flag.

Corporal, 6th Pennsylvania Cavalry (Rush's Lancers)

Raised as the 70th Volunteers, the 6th Pennsylvania Cavalry (Rush's Lancers) were named after their Colonel, Richard H. Rush. The uniform was basically of the regulation style, with dark blue trousers being worn early in the regiment's existence; a photograph taken at Falmouth, Virginia, in 1862 shows them to have been replaced by the more conventional light blue. The regiment wore one loop of lace on the collar (the distinguishing mark of volunteer cavalry); the brass shoulder-scales were soon discarded. Officers wore the crossed sabres badge on the front of the képi, the other ranks having theirs on the crown. On the carbine-belt was worn an unusual brass oval-shaped plate with pointed ends, bearing the device of crossed lances crudely-stamped into the metal.

The regiment took its name from their principal arm: nine-feet long lances of Norwegian fir. Finally being accepted as unserviceable in May 1863, the lances were replaced by sabres and carbines.

The leather-covered wooden McClellan saddle was held in place by a girth and surcingle of blue webbing. Stirrups were wooden, covered with leather and including large leather 'hoods' which all but covered the rider's foot. Horse-furniture was generally of black leather with brass fittings and steel bit; the blanket under the saddle was often dark blue with a broad orange stripe near the edge, with 'U.S.' in orange letters at the centre, though grey blankets with yellow trim were not uncommon. On the saddle was carried a canvas nosebag, rolled overcoat, blanket, two black leather saddlebags containing rations, ammunition, clothing, horseshoes and other equipment and a thirty-feet long lariat.

Officer, 3rd Pennsylvania Cavalry (60th Volunteers); Officer, 4th Pennsylvania Cavalry (64th Volunteers)

This plate illustrates two of the typical unorthodox uniforms adopted by officers on campaign: they are taken from photographs of the staffs of Colonel W. W. Averell of the 3rd Pennsylvania Cavalry (Young's Kentucky Light Cavalry – 60th Volunteers), and of Colonel J. E. Childe of the 4th Pennsylvania Cavalry (64th Volunteers).

The officer of the 3rd wears a half-military, half-civilian costume, only the dark blue jacket indicating to which army he belongs. Even in this case, no badges of rank are worn, and the civilian hat and bow-tie appear somewhat incongruous when coupled with the sabre and pistol.

The officer of the 4th wears a regulation hat, battered almost beyond recognition, and a long blue coat with breast-pocket (from which a handkerchief protrudes), gauntlets, striped shirt and white collar. Both original photographs from which this plate is taken include other officers dressed in more regulation styles, with képis and shell-jackets, though another officer of the 4th wears the same type of long coat, over a dark waistcoat, white shirt and collar, and large dark bow-tie.

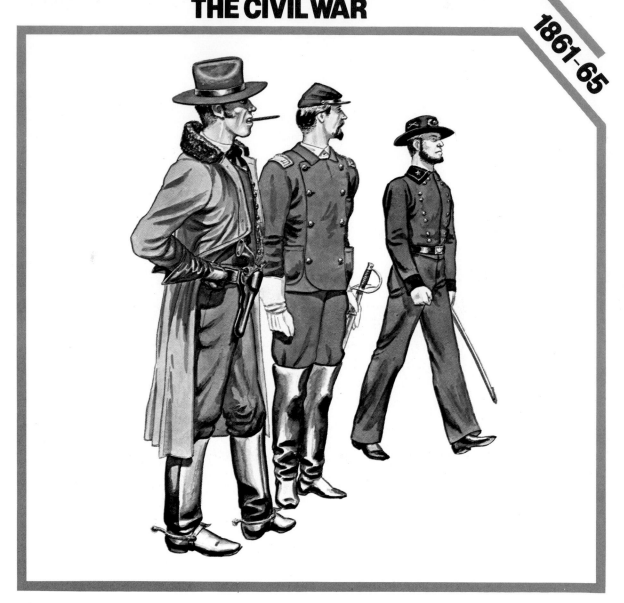

Officer, 1st Cavalry; Officer, 9th Vermont Cavalry; General of Cavalry

The figures on this plate (all taken from contemporary photographs) show variations of the cavalry uniform as worn on campaign. The officer of the 1st U.S. Cavalry wears a civilian, fur-collared overcoat and civilian hat, with no visible badges of rank, only his pistol identifying him as a soldier.

The officer of the 9th Vermont Cavalry wears a type of 'patrol jacket', the other items of uniform being of the regulation pattern.

The General of Cavalry, taken from a photograph of Brigadier-

General A. T. A. Torbert of Sheridan's staff, shows a uniform probably designed by the officer himself. The wearer's rank is indicated by the arrangement of the buttons and the rank-star worn on the collar and 'slouch' hat.

This pattern of uniform was worn by other General officers: Custer wore a black velvet version with blue collar and Confederate-style cuff lacing, black breeches with gold stripe, with either a képi or black 'slouch' hat, the whole covered with yards of gold braid.

While few officers approached this sartorial level, completely-regulation uniforms were few and

far between in the later stages of the War.

THE CIVIL WAR

Private, 4th U.S. Cavalry, Dress Uniform, 1862

Companies A and E of the 4th served as escorts for Major General George B. McClellan when he commanded the Army of the Potomac. Then white gloves and shoulder scales were the rule. Note the brass insignia on the forage cap. The 4th was armed with the Model 1852 Sharps carbine, the Model 1860 Colt Army revolver and the U.S. Model 1860 light cavalry sabre.

Private, 5th U.S. Cavalry, Undress, 1862

Contrary to popular belief, the enlisted man's overcoat did not actually receive a yellow lining until the 1880s. This fellow wears a mashed up 'Hardee' hat and has tucked his trousers into his boots – an increasingly common practice. In 1862 the 5th Cavalry carried Sharps carbines, Colt Army revolvers and U.S. Model 1840 sabres.

Corporal, 1st U.S. Cavalry, Undress, 1862

First introduced to the cavalry in 1858, the four-button sack coat (or fatigue blouse) saw extensive service in the Civil War and after. Forage caps were often worn without insignia. The 1st Cavalry fought with Smith carbines, Colt Army revolvers and U.S. Model 1860 sabres in 1862. Both regulars and volunteers turned out in an endless variety of enlisted dress. This cross-section of Yankee cavalry uniforms is based on contemporary records, photographs and sketches.

Officer, Infantry, Campaign Dress; Sergeant, 2nd Infantry, Full Dress; Officer, Infantry, Full Dress

The regulation 'Hardee' hat, complete with plume, was worn in full dress by infantry officers, the badge on the front consisting of an embroidered hunting-horn badge (with or without regimental identification). The frock-coat was double-breasted for field officers (i.e. from Major to Colonel), having two rows of buttons, seven in each, spaced equally. In full dress, epaulettes of a similar pattern to those of the cavalry were worn; otherwise, the same uniform was worn with embroidered rank-bars on the shoulders. Commissioned rank was further indicated by the universal red sash; either gloves or gauntlets were worn. Trousers (officially dark blue) were more often light blue with an ⅛th-inch wide seam-stripe.

On campaign, officers adopted numerous non-regulation variations; that illustrated is taken from a contemporary photograph. The képi bears a similar badge to that worn on the full-dress hat; the short jacket bears rank-bars and is worn with collar, tie and waistcoat. Officers' waistcoats were officially dark blue, white or buff with nine buttons and standing or 'rolled' collar, but numerous variations existed.

Other ranks wore a single-breasted frock-coat in full dress, piped with the infantry distinguishing colour (light blue), with brass shoulder-scales. The cords on the 'Hardee' hat were of the same colour as the piping. The badge of the hunting-horn with regimental and company identification was in brass for other ranks, borne on the front of the hat; when the hat was replaced with the képi for active service, these badges were transferred until discarded completely (as they frequently were).

Private, 20th Maine; Corporal, Iron Brigade, First Uniform; Private, Iron Brigade, Service Dress

The private of the 20th Maine illustrated wears the ordinary fatigue uniform, but with the official regulation dark blue trousers; the regiment was one of the few to adhere to the original trousers rather than adopt the light blue ones authorised in December 1861. The figure shows the regulation infantry equipment, consisting of a waist-belt and small cap-pouch to the right of the brass plate, and a shoulder-belt supporting the cartridge-pouch on the right hip, the pouch having a tin liner and often a brass plate.

The original uniforms of the Brigade were of the typical volunteer grey; the grey uniform of the 2nd Wisconsin caused considerable confusion at First Bull Run when the regiment was forced to retire in disorder, having confused the Confederate army with their own!

By September 1861 all the grey costumes had been replaced by dark blue frock-coats, 'Hardee' hats, light blue trousers and white gaiters; thus originated their nickname of 'The Black Hat Brigade'. This was the classic uniform of the Brigade, though the ravages of campaigning soon took

their toll: by 1863 the frock-coat had been replaced by the fatigue-coat in perhaps half the brigade, though photographs show the two being worn even within the same company.

Private, 21st Michigan, Service Dress; Private, Irish Brigade; Private, 8th Wisconsin, Service Dress

The figures of the 21st Michigan and 8th Wisconsin (both taken from contemporary photographs) show typical variations of the campaign uniform. The 21st Michigan almost entirely wore battered black 'slouch' hats with or without leather bands; the fatigue-blouse in this case worn with the top button unfastened and the lapels turned back, though a number of full dress frock-coats were also worn.

The 8th Wisconsin apparently largely retained the frock-coat with the ubiquitous battered hat. The regiment was known as 'The Eagle Regiment' from their custom of taking the regimental mascot — an eagle — into battle with them, sitting on a specially-constructed perch.

The Irish Brigade (1st Division, II Corps, Army of the Potomac) was originally composed of the 63rd, 69th and 88th New York, being the 3rd, 1st and 4th/5th Regiments of Thomas Francis Meagher's Irish Brigade respectively, being raised from Irish immigrants in New York by Meagher, who had been transported from Ireland to Tasmania in 1852 for treason and sedition. The Brigade especially distinguished itself at Fredericksburg and Antietam.

The Irish Brigade wore a distinctive uniform, consisting of the regulation fatigue coat with the addition of green collars and cuffs, and grey trousers; the badge worn on top of the képi was a red clover-leaf. To emphasise their Irish origin, each regiment carried a green flag in addition to their regulation colours.

Officer, 5th New York Zouaves, Full Dress; Zouave, Campaign Dress; Private, 5th New York Zouaves, Full Dress

Mustered into service on 9 May 1861 for a two-year enlistment, the 5th New York (Duryée Zouaves) was one of the best units to serve in the Union army.

The Zouaves fashion sprang into favour before the outbreak of the war, when drill-teams dressed to resemble the élite French light infantry gave public displays throughout the country. Volunteer and militia companies copied the style extensively. The 5th New York wore a typical Zouave costume: fez with white turban wound round for parade, the blue tasselled cap being worn alone on service. The rank and file wore the conventional Zouave jacket and shirt, with 'baggy' trousers tucked into high gaiters. In common with most Zouave units, officers wore a modified version of the regulation uniform, basically, the frock-coat with Confederate-style cuff-braid, red képi and trousers.

Despite their reputation, British war correspondent William Howard Russell (who had seen the genuine French Zouaves) was unimpressed by the 5th New York; some men wore the turban without the fez underneath, so that their hair stuck through the 'discoloured napkins', while Russell considered the trousers – 'loose bags of red calico' – to be quite 'ridiculous', the net effect being a line of military 'scarecrows'. A less critical eye, however, would have been most impressed with the regiment's colour-guard, many of whom were approaching seven feet in height.

The Zouave officer in campaign dress (taken from a contemporary photograph) shows how the uniform was modified on campaign; only the stocking-cap identifies the man as a member of a Zouave unit.

79th New York Volunteers, 1861; Private, Full Dress; Private, Service Dress; Sergeant, Full Dress

Formed at the suggestion of Captain Roderick of the British Consulate on 9 October 1859, this regiment of New York State Militia took its name and number from the 79th (Cameron) Highlanders of the British army, its four companies being composed of Scottish immigrants.

In full dress a Scottish doublet was worn, with red shoulder-straps bearing the numerals '79' in brass, red cuff-patches piped light blue, with collar of either red edged light blue, or light blue with red and white patch. The rear tails of the doublet bore embroidered yellow grenades. With this uniform was worn a Glengarry cap in full dress, with diced border and brass badge; there was a regimental badge prior to the war, but this was later replaced by a replica of the State seal. Kilts and truibhs (trews) were worn in full dress, of Cameron of Erracht tartan like those of their counterparts in the British army. With the kilt was worn a white hair sporran with black 'tails' and a white metal thistle badge, diced hose, red garters and black shoes with silver buckles. N.C.O.s wore red sashes and yellow epaulettes; chevrons were light blue and their swords were of a typically-Scottish pattern.

The regulation képi was also worn, having a brass badge in the form of a hunting horn with '79' in the centre; the equipment was of the standard U.S. issue. The Scottish costume soon disappeared when active campaigning began, like the more exotic costume of other volunteer regiments; even before First Bull Run many had abandoned the kilt for the regulation light blue trousers as illustrated.

Private, 7th New York National Guard; Corporal, 7th New York National Guard; Sergeant, New York Militia

Tracing their descent to 1806, the title of the 7th New York National Guard was adopted by the Regiment in 1847. An active force in city riot-control, the more unruly members of the mob christened the 7th 'the old greybacks', their dislike of the part-time soldiers being increased by the fact that all ranks were drawn from the highest-ranked members of the community, enlistment in the 7th being considered more like an exclusive club. Under the command of Abram

Duryée (later of Zouave fame) from 1849 to 1859 the regiment became the most famous 'civilian' corps in the country.

The uniform of the 7th was of the typical pre-war militia style, consisting of képi, shell-jacket and trousers of light grey with black trimming. The képi bore the company number on the front in a small brass numeral. The brass waist-belt plate bore the initials 'N.G.' and the company number (in letters); the cypher 'N.G.' was repeated in ornate lettering in the cartridge-pouch. Equipment consisted of canteen, knapsack, leather-covered mess-pail strapped

to the rear of the knapsack, and a red blanket. White leather equipment was worn from 1849 until 1861. In 1853 shakos were issued, but these were reserved for full dress. Greatcoats were light blue; the regiment was armed with the 1855 Rifle musket.

The third figure on this plate (taken from a contemporary painting) shows the influence of French styles in the uniform of another New York Militia corps.

THE CIVIL WAR

Officer, 1st Rhode Island Volunteers; Private, 1st Rhode Island Volunteers; Private, 2nd New Hampshire Volunteers

The 1st Rhode Island Volunteers was organised around Providence, and commanded by Ambrose Everett Burnside, later to become General. The 1st Rhode Island served at First Bull Run.

The uniform was remarkably different from other Union volunteer corps, both 1st and 2nd Rhode Island wearing at least two and possibly three distinct styles of blouse, known as 'Burnside' or 'Rhode Island' blouses. One, of plain blue cloth, very nearly resembled the classic 'hunting shirt' beloved of American 'backwoodsmen' for generations; another similar blouse with a pleated front and very wide collar was referred to as a 'hunting jacket'; the third was of the same length but with a buttoned-on 'plastron' front and standing collar, probably inspired by the dress of the numerous volunteer fire-fighting companies from which many volunteer regiments were raised. Trousers were either grey or light blue; the red blanket, normally worn rolled across the body, could be worn as a 'poncho' by means of a slit cut in the middle to act as a neck-hole. The officer illustrated is carrying a Beaumont-Adams revolver.

The 2nd New Hampshire Volunteers served in Burnside's Brigade at First Bull Run.

The regiment wore one of the most archaic uniforms of the war in the early months of its service, consisting of a long tailcoat with red turnbacks, lining, and piping, the whole being of volunteer grey. Leather equipment was apparently either white or black. Officers probably wore a similar style of dress, or perhaps the more regulation dark blue frock-coat.

Sergeant with marker flag, 14th New York Volunteers; Sergeant, Company 'D', 19th Illinois Volunteers (Ellsworth Zouave Cadets)

Ephraim Elmer Ellsworth (after whom Company 'D' of the 19th Illinois was named as Ellsworth's Zouave Cadets) could be considered the instigator of the 'Zouave movement' in America.

The 14th New York Militia (later 84th New York Infantry [The Brooklyn Chasseurs]) were uniformed to resemble the Chasseurs à Pied (light infantry) of the French army, though contemporary reports of 'red-legged zouaves' of the 14th at Antietam confused the two French styles. The képi of the 14th bore the numerals '14' on the front, and was further distinguished by the blue circle on the crown. Though the jacket appeared to have been worn over a red shirt, the jacket and 'shirt' were in fact one garment, the blue sewn onto the red, the buttons on the blue being purely decorative. The detachable 'trefoil' epaulettes were worn by all ranks; the canvas gaiters buttoned up the side. The waistbelt cap-pouch was ornamented with a brass State device consisting of an eagle with outstretched wings over a shield, over a scroll; the waist-belt plate bore the device 'S.N.Y.' ('State of New York', interpreted by the Confederates as 'Snotty-Nosed Yanks'!) Officers wore a more regulation uniform or frock-coat, but with the regimental red trousers which had a gold lace stripe down the outer seam.

The sergeant is carrying a marker flag attached to the muzzle of his rifle; these small standards were used to enable the men to keep their 'dressing' in action; based upon the National flag, the blue canton contained the regimental number surrounded by thirteen stars of the colonies.

Sharpshooters; Officer and Corporal

The uniform of the two Sharpshooter regiments was as unusual as their rôle. The dark green képi was decorated with badges of brass crossed rifles with the letters 'S.S.' and 'U.S.' worn on occasion by the rank and file, whilst officers wore the letters 'U.S.S.S.' surrounded by a wreath in gold embroidery on the crown of the cap. Corps badges were later worn on the képi: a red diamond for example when the Sharpshooters formed part of the 1st Division, III Corps. In full dress a black feather plume was worn on the cap, and often black, brown or grey 'slouch' hats on campaign. The dark green frock-coats were worn by all ranks, N.C.O.s' chevrons being either light blue or dark green on a light blue patch. Trousers were originally light blue, but were later changed to green to match the rest of the uniform and were often worn with long black or brown leather gaiters. Officers wore crimson sashes; equipment was of black leather, though knapsacks were made of goatskin with the hair left on. Cartridge-pouches bore oval brass plates with the letters 'U.S.' embossed (the same design as the belt-plates) and were carried by all ranks, officers being armed with rifles in addition to the usual pistol. Greatcoats were either grey (sometimes trimmed with dark green) or light blue; equipment was usually discarded in action to allow maximum freedom of movement. Non-reflective rubber buttons were used at one time.

In addition to the Sharps rifle, a number of .56 Colt revolving rifles were used, these being most unpopular due to the tendency of blowing up in the face of the owner! Some selected marksmen carried heavy, precision-made snipers' rifles with telescopic sights for even greater accuracy.

Sergeant, 1st Heavy Artillery, Corps d'Afrique; 1st Sergeant, 56th U.S. Colored Infantry; Private, U.S. Colored Infantry

The 1st Heavy Artillery of the Corps d'Afrique (previously the 1st Louisiana Heavy Artillery [African Descent]), formed part of the garrison of New Orleans. Their uniform was basically the artillery full dress, with the battery identification letter borne above the crossed cannons badge on the hat. The New Orleans sector being comparatively quiet, the troops there were able to maintain their uniforms near to the full dress regulations, never having to succumb to the more ragged appearance of their more heavily-engaged comrades in other theatres of war. The sidearm was the 1833 pattern Foot Artillery sword, a copy of the French weapon originally based on the ancient Roman gladius.

Other black regiments wore standard fatigue uniform with no special distinctions, except that in many cases many regiments received uniforms of excellent quality, the normal coarse cloth having temporarily run out at the time the coloured regiments were raised. This plate illustrates two variations, both taken from contemporary photographs. The private wears the regulation full-dress frock-coat with the collar turned down, and has a képi covered in a black 'waterproof', a common addition in wet weather. The 1st Sergeant of the 56th Coloured Infantry (originally the 3rd Arkansas Infantry [African Descent]) wears what appears to be a shell-jacket, but which was, in fact, a cut-down frock-coat (note the piping on collar and cuffs).

1st Lieutenant, 2nd Artillery, Service Dress, 1862; 1st Lieutenant, 14th Ohio Volunteer Light Artillery, 1864; Gunner, Light Artillery, Full Dress

The U.S. Artillery was divided into two branches, Artillery and Light Artillery.

In uniform, however, there was a much clearer distinction, the light artillery having a style of dress corresponding to that of their European counterparts. The blue cloth shako with hanging plume and red cords bore a brass crossed-cannons badge on the front, together with a U.S. shield badge. The remainder of the uniform,

consisting of shell-jacket and trousers (cut loose to spread over the boot) was in obvious cavalry style, whilst maintaining the red distinctive colour in the form of piping.

As with other branches of the army, the service uniform for officers of artillery consisted of frock-coat with rank bars, light blue trousers with red stripe, either képi or felt hat, and crimson silk sash. The uniform of the 14th Ohio Light Artillery illustrated (taken from a photograph of 1st Lieutenant Thomas Jeffery) shows a variation on this uniform; the hat-badge consisted of crossed cannon-

barrels instead of the prescribed gold-embroidered cannon with silver regimental number beneath, on a backing of black velvet; the sash was omitted, and a black leather telescope-case was hung from one shoulder.

The other figure (taken from photographs of Lieutenant-Colonel William Hays and 1st Lieutenant William N. Dennison of the 2nd Artillery) wears a more unorthodox fatigue blouse with rank-bars sewn on, with shirt and scarf underneath. Not all officers carried sabres, but the pistol was an almost universal sidearm. Buff gauntlets were common to all officers.

Private, 4th New Hampshire Regiment; Private, 22nd New York Regiment; Captain, Invalid Corps.
In April 1863 the Invalid Corps was established, consisting of officers and men of the Union army unfit for full combat duty due to injury or illness but who could perform limited infantry service. A total of twenty-four regiments and 188 separate companies were established, who performed guard and garrison duty to relieve front-line soldiers. The name was changed on 18 March 1864 to The Veteran Reserve Corps, as the previous initial of the Invalid Corps coincided with those stamped on

worn-out equipment and animals ('Inspected – Condemned'), which had caused some friction within the corps! Officers wore the regulation képi, sky-blue frock-coats with dark blue rank-bars, and sky blue trousers with two dark blue stripes down the seam; other ranks had képis and trousers like the regular army, but sky blue 'jersey jackets cut long in the waist' and trimmed with dark blue. This uniform was extremely unpopular as the members of the Invalid Corps disliked such obvious distinction from the 'real soldiers' fit for active service. Regular troops also were jealous of the Invalids who had

easier tasks. Eventually officers of the Veteran Reserve Corps were allowed to wear the normal dark blue frock-coat.

The 4th New Hampshire Infantry wore, for a period, a 'pith helmet' or sun helmet, designed to protect the wearer from the heat of the sun. Such helmets were not uncommon (particularly in the earlier part of the war), and were privately-purchased by many officers as well as being issued to certain regiments. The 22nd New York (Union Greys) wore militia-style grey uniforms with red facings and white piping, the whole uniform being styled to resemble the French type of costume.

Confederate General, Full Dress; Major, Engineers, Full Dress; Brigadier-General

Confederate General officers wore a frock-coat for full dress, not dissimilar to that of the Federal regulations, but of grey, with buff facing-colour on the collar, cuffs and piping. Their buttons were arranged in pairs, eight per row. Rank was indicated by an embroidered badge on either side of the collar, consisting of three stars within a laurel wreath, by cuff-lacing of four thicknesses wide, and by the buff waist-sash. A small bicorn 'chapeau' was authorised for full dress wear, but in practice

seems to have been worn even less than its Federal counterpart, plain 'slouch' hats being preferred by the majority; otherwise, a dark blue képi with gold lace decorations four thicknesses wide was worn. Trousers were dark blue with two ⅝th-inch wide stripes of gold lace down the outer seams. Another popular garment was a frock-coat more resembling a civilian overcoat, worn open to expose the waistcoat (this figure is taken from a photograph of G. W. C. Lee). Rank-badges were frequently worn on the turned-back lapels of such coats. As in many other cases, self-designed uniforms or even civilian

clothes were far more common on active service than regulation costume.

The Major of Engineers illustrated wears the officially-prescribed full dress uniform with low 'chapeau' with gold star badge on the right-hand side, gold lace band and transverse plume of black ostrich feathers. Facings for the Engineer Corps were buff like those of the Staff, but the sash was red. The buttons on the frock-coat were arranged in the pattern authorised for all except general officers: i.e. single-spaced.

THE CIVIL WAR

Major, Cavalry; General of Cavalry

Though officially required to wear the regulation frock-coat, many Confederate cavalry officers preferred short jackets, often double-breasted with yellow-lined lapels which could be buttoned back to give the garment an almost eighteenth-century appearance. Collar, cuffs and piping were also in the yellow distinctive colour of the cavalry, with rank badges and cuff-lacing as per regulations. Underneath the jacket was worn any type of waistcoat, shirt and cravat. Officially, the képi was the prescribed headgear, but hats, usually black or grey in colour,

were by far the most common form of head-dress. Most officers wore the regulation yellow silk sash, and white or buff gauntlets were very popular. According to regulations, trousers were light blue with a 1¼-inch wide yellow stripe down the outer seam, but grey or other colours were not uncommon, while buff corduroy as illustrated was perhaps the most popular of all.

Most Confederate cavalry officers carried a sabre of varying pattern: the version illustrated could be either a captured Federal weapon, a Confederate copy of the same, or a European import: straight-bladed imported weapons

were also in common usage. The sword was supported on black leather slings from the waist-belt, which sometimes had an extra support in the form of a narrow shoulder-belt, not unlike the famous British 'Sam Browne' belt adopted later in the century. The pistol was a universal sidearm, that illustrated being a copy of the Colt 'Dragoon' revolver, manufactured by J. H. Dance and Bros.

The General officer of cavalry wears a uniform basically of a cavalry style, but with appropriate rank-badges on the collar, and General's cuff-lace and button-arrangement.

THE CIVIL WAR

Private, Cavalry, Campaign Dress
This plate shows a typical Confederate trooper of about 1863, before the most severe shortages of uniforms and equipment led to the virtual disappearance of anything resembling regulation styles. Though many militia units had good horse-furniture of pre-war vintage, there was little uniformity in the type of saddle used, varying from the U.S. McClellan pattern or its Confederate copy, the older Grimsley and Jennifer patterns, with numerous imported models and civilian saddles. A large number of Model 1842 and Model 1850 U.S. Dragoon bits were used, as well as numerous imported varieties, but harnessing was in most cases much simpler than that used by the Federals. Saddle-bags were often replaced by small canvas bags or sacks, and any available material served as saddle-blankets. Stirrups were either wooden or, more popularly, heavy cast brass, as well as numerous non-regulation varieties. Bosses and decorations (where they existed at all) were usually of plain brass, though some existed with 'C.S.' or 'C.S.A.' stamped on.

The trooper illustrated wears a regulation shell-jacket with yellow facings, but with the customary 'slouch' hat replacing the képi. Equipment is carried on the saddle-blanket, rolled greatcoat, canteen and cloth haversack — as was on occasion the sword. The trooper is armed with an imported 'Prussian'-style straight-bladed sabre with brass hilt, and a carbine; pistols were extremely popular and it was not unusual for a shotgun to be carried in place of the carbine.

Corporal, Cavalry, Full Dress, with Guidon; Sergeant, 1st Virginia Cavalry

The Confederate regulation cavalry uniform consisted of a double-breasted frock-coat with yellow facings and trimming, and two rows of seven buttons on the breast. N.C.O.s wore yellow chevrons and 1¾-inch stripes on the outer seams of their light blue trousers; senior N.C.O.s were officially supposed to wear yellow sashes, but in practice these were almost non-existent. The regulation képi was yellow with a dark blue band. However, very few uniforms conformed to these regulations, the prescribed items being replaced by hats, shell-jackets, double-breasted fatigue-blouses or Federal-style fatigue dress, with or without facings and piping. Musicians were supposed to have yellow lace on the breast but this was seldom (if ever) worn. The corporal illustrated in this plate wears a uniform conforming almost exactly to the official regulations, except the rectangular belt-plate bearing 'C.S.' has been replaced by a plain brass buckle, a very popular style.

The guidon carried is based upon the first National flag, with a variation in the placement of the stars, six small ones being grouped around a larger one. Other variations existed, including one with seven four-pointed stars arranged in three rows.

The 1st Virginia was uniformed in 'Hussar' style, their grey shell-jackets being faced and braided with black. Unusually for regiments wearing this type of braid, N.C.O.s' chevrons were yellow. The fashionable long hair, beards and plumed 'slouch' hats gave the regiment a deliberately-acquired 'cavalier' style. Not all the companies wore black shoulder-straps.

Sergeant, 1st Texas Cavalry, 1861; Private, Charleston Light Dragoons, 1860

Raised from independent volunteer companies in South Carolina, the 4th South Carolina Cavalry (Rutledge Cavalry) contained the Charleston Light Dragoons (Rutledge Rangers), as Company 'K'. The splendid, almost Napoleonic, uniform included the ornate leather and brass dragoon helmet, which bore the State emblem – the Palmetto tree – on a rosette at each side of the helmet, and on the front plate, which being a crescent-shaped device, itself repeated another of the emblems found on the South

Carolina flag; the Palmetto tree was also stamped on the waist-belt plate. This magnificent uniform, however, was reserved for full dress occasions, being replaced by grey fatigue uniforms (issued in December 1860) for active service.

The 1st Texas Cavalry (also known as the Texas Mounted Rifles or Partisan Rangers), though uniformed in a basically-regulation style, had black facings on the shell-jackets and the unusual cuff-flaps; as in many other Texan units, the 'Lone Star' device was much in evidence. The 1st Texas served in Fitzburgh Lee's Brigade; it should not be confused with the other

Partisan Rangers (5th North Carolina Cavalry), or with Companies 'F' and 'H' of the 2nd Texas Cavalry, both known as the Texas Mounted Riflemen.

The sergeant is illustrated examining a captured Federal regulation-issue 'McClellan' saddle.

Private, 26th Texas Cavalry (Debray's Mounted Riflemen); Private, Texas Cavalry, with Guidon; Private, 1st Kentucky Cavalry Brigade

The 26th Texas Cavalry, also known as Debray's Mounted Riflemen, was uniformed and armed in a typically French fashion, the regulation cavalry dress having green facings and piping, brass shoulder-scales, and brass numerals '26' on the collars of N.C.O.s and privates. Musicians wore the usual pattern of lacing on the breast, but in the unusual green colour. It is not certain, however, whether this uniform was ever issued to any

members of the regiment other than to Debray and his second-in-command. The 26th were armed with Mexican lances with yellow and blue pennons; these were a dubious advantage, and were replaced in October 1862 by Enfield rifles and revolvers.

The Confederate cavalry greatcoat was double-breasted with standing collar and brass buttons, the cape long enough to reach the cuffs of the coat, the whole being grey in colour. It is doubtful, however, whether many such overcoats conformed exactly to regulations, a wide variety of styles and designs being used. The

private illustrated wears the official pattern, and has the distinctive all-yellow képi of the 1st Kentucky Cavalry Brigade.

The Texan cavalryman wears a simple all-grey uniform, the yellow facing colour being borne only on the collar; the guidon is the 'Lone Star' State flag, carried in this shape by Texan cavalry units.

The Kentucky cavalryman is shown armed with a Deane and Adams revolver fitted with a Kerr patent ramrod.

Private, 8th Texas Cavalry. Campaign Dress; Private, Regulation Dress

The Texas Rangers were originally raised during the War of Texan Independence. Reorganised by Sam Houston, the Ranger companies acted as State Militia during the Civil War, but their name was transferred to the 8th Texas Cavalry, raised by B. F. Terry and Thomas S. Lubbock, generally known as the 1st Texas Rangers or 'Terry's Texas Rangers'.

Officially, the uniform consisted of grey képi with yellow band, light grey shell-jacket with yellow facings, and dark grey trousers with yellow stripe down the outer seam. The rigours of campaigning and the shortages of material compelled the regiment to dress in whatever clothing they could find or steal – captured Federal items, black or grey 'slouch' hat, coloured scarf; brown, grey or blue jackets with or without red facings; trousers of any colour, many captured from the Union; in fact any item of clothing was pressed into service, being given 'uniformity' by the addition of scarlet trimming when possible. Wearing such costume had its dangers: on 5 January 1864 Private E. S. Dodd of the 8th Texas was shot by the Union as a spy, having been captured wearing items of Federal uniform! As popular with most Texan units, the 'Lone Star' emblem of the State was always in evidence on belt-plates, accoutrements and head-dress; Company 'F', in fact, was known as the 'Lone Star Rangers'.

Serving in the West, the 8th Texas had a fine record, and in the 1870's the Texas Rangers were reorganised as a police force to patrol and protect against bandits and Indians; they continue as an independent police force to the present day, maintaining the high record of their forebears.

Major, Infantry, Full Dress; Colonel, 20th Alabama Regiment; 2nd Lieutenant, Infantry, Campaign Dress

In full dress, Confederate infantry officers wore the regulation frock-coat with light blue facings and trimming, though all-grey uniforms were not uncommon. Rank-lacing on the cuffs and rank-badges on the collar were of gold lace; buttons were gilt. The képi was officially light blue with dark blue band and gold lace, though it appeared in a combination of light and dark blue and grey as well. Trousers were light blue with a 1¾-inch dark blue stripe; rank was further distinguished by the red silk sash worn under the waistbelt.

On campaign, the uniform frequently underwent radical alteration: though the frock-coat was retained in many cases, shorter jackets like those worn by the rank and file were popular. The képi was frequently replaced by a 'slouch' hat, commonly black, with or without decorative feather plumes. Trousers were often grey or blue-grey, sometimes worn with knee-boots as illustrated. The sash was frequently discarded, and often a pistol alone was carried, the sword not being universally popular. Overcoats, when used, were like those of the other ranks, though numerous non-regulation styles existed.

The officer of the 20th Alabama Infantry illustrated (based upon a contemporary photograph) wears the standard infantry uniform, with the addition of felt hat with turned-up brim. Isham W. Garrot, Colonel of the 20th, was promoted Brigadier-General (28 May 1863); he was killed by a sharpshooter at Vicksburg on 17 June 1863.

The 2nd Lieutenant illustrated is armed with an ornate, pearl-handled Navy Colt revolver.

**Private, Infantry, Full Dress;
Sergeant-Major, Infantry, Full Dress**

This plate shows the regulation full dress of enlisted men of the Confederate infantry, though it is doubtful whether many were ever issued (if at all); it is possible that the uniform never went beyond the prototype stage, as materials ran short after the opening months of the war.

According to the manual 'Uniforms and Dress of the Army of the Confederate States' issued in September 1861 by Adjutant- and Inspector-General Samuel Cooper, it is possible that the regulation head-dress was intended to be a shako similar to the 1851 pattern of the U.S. Army, possibly of black, dark blue or grey cloth, with pompom and presumably brass plate;however, the regulations are so vague that the pattern of shako or whatever cannot be determined and in any case 'General Order No. 4' of January 1862 authorised the use of the forage cap (képi) to be worn by all ranks in full dress,the top to be light blue, with a dark blue band.

The grey frock-coat was to extend half-way between the knees and hips, double-breasted, with two rows of seven buttons and light blue facings and piping; N.C.O.s' rank chevrons and sashes (the latter worn when the sword was carried) were to be of the light blue distinguishing colour also. Trousers were to be light blue, with a 1¼-inch dark blue stripe for N.C.O.s; musicians were to have Federal-style light blue froggings on the breast of the coat, and a light blue sash. All equipment was to be of black leather. The brass infantry badge (a hunting horn) was officially to be worn on the top of the képi and, if possible, the regimental number on the front of the cap; but it seems extremely unlikely that any of these devices were ever actually worn.

1861-65

Private, Infantry, Service Dress
This plate illustrates two versions of the semi-regulation service uniform worn by the rank and file of the Confederate infantry, before the shortages of material led to the complete degeneration of uniform into semi-civilian and home-dyed costume.

The authorised fatigue uniform consisted of a grey double-breasted, blouse with two rows of seven buttons but it seems likely that the single-breasted version illustrated was more common. This uniform was worn with or without light blue facings, and occasionally 'slash'-type cuffs were worn in place of the authorised pointed variety. Trousers were the regulation light blue, sometimes captured from the Federals.

Before the wearing of the brimmed hat became almost universal, the colouring of the képi was changed to grey with a band of light blue, and all-grey képis were not uncommon. As supplies became scarcer, the fatigue coat was often replaced by a grey shell-jacket, often worn without any facings, or with just the collar of light blue. Grey trousers were worn with or without a light blue stripe down the outer seams. Equipment, originally of black leather, gradually became brown or 'natural' in colour as black dye became scarcer. Much Federal equipment was captured and pressed into service, a favourite trick being to wear the Union waist-belt with the 'u.s.' plate upside-down.

Corporal, Infantry, with 1st National Flag; Private, Infantry, with Battle Flag

The corporal illustrated wears an all-grey Federal-style fatigue uniform of Confederate grey, with only the chevrons in the infantry distinctive colour, and knapsack replaced by a green civilian blanket. His colour is the First National Flag of the Confederacy (adopted 4 March 1861), known as the 'Stars and Bars' from the three large stripes and from the seven white stars arranged in a circle on the blue canton.

The private is notable because he wears not a single item of regulation equipment, a common state of affairs as the war moved into its later stages and materials became progressively more scarce. The straw hat, unbleached cotton shirt, neckerchief and 'natural' leather belts are all civilian items, while the trousers and 'gum blanket' shoulder-roll are captured Union items. The pistol carried is a Starr .44 revolver. The Confederate Battle Flag as illustrated consisted of a dark blue saltaire cross on a red field, edged white, the cross bearing thirteen white stars.

Confederate colour-bearers were (according to regulations) to wear a badge of crossed flags on the arm to signify their appointment, but due to the high casualty-rate among colour-parties in many cases not only this badge but also the colour-belt was not worn.

Sergeant, Texas Infantry, with State Flag, 1863; Sergeant-Major, South Carolina Volunteers, with State Flag, 1861

Many Confederate units carried the Flags of their native State; two such are illustrated in this plate. The South Carolina flag, with blue background bearing the State emblems of Crescent moon and Palmetto tree, was that finally adopted on secession; prior to this (1860–61), South Carolina units carried a red flag bearing a dark blue cross with vertical and horizontal arms; at the intersection of the arms was a large white star. On each of the horizontal arms were four smaller stars, and three on each of the vertical arms; the crescent and Palmetto tree appeared in white in the upper canton nearest the pole.

Texan units carried the familiar flag. Other State banners varied considerably: Virginian units, for example, carried a blue flag bearing the State seal in the centre; the North Carolina design was like that of Texas, but with a white star on a red bar, and white over blue stripes. Arkansas units often carried Battle Flags of a plain white cross on blue field.

The South Carolinan sergeant-major wears a uniform typical of those of the early volunteer corps, consisting of shell-jacket, képi and trousers, of plain grey with light blue chevrons and sash. The belt-plate bears the Palmetto Tree emblem; the regulation shoulder-belt to support the butt of the colour-pole was worn over one shoulder. The Texan sergeant also wears the State emblem, having the 'Lone Star' badge on hat and belt-plate. The fashion of wearing the shell jacket fastened by only one button at the neck, hanging open to expose the shirt, was a very popular style.

THE CIVIL WAR

Private, Sumter Light Guard; Bass Drummer, Sumter Light Guard; Officer, Sumter Light Guard

The figures on this plate are based upon a photograph taken in April 1861 of the Sumter Light Guard (Company 'K', 4th Georgia Volunteers); being in black and white, it is difficult to be precise as to the exact colouring of the uniforms. The company wore dark uniforms (képi, shell-jacket and trousers) with light-coloured shoulder-straps and trouser-stripes, officers being distinguished by frock-coats, sashes, knee-boots and the broad white shoulder-belt. Equipment appears to have been of

standard Federal pattern, though it is likely that some form of State device was worn upon the belt-plates. The drummer appears to be wearing an almost civilian-style 'uniform', with large bow-tie and shirt-collar visible beneath the turned-back lapels of the jacket, and a remarkably battered felt hat turned up at the front.

Other details (common to many Confederate volunteer corps) are shown on the photograph but not illustrated. Shirt-collars and even ties show above the shell-jacket collars of many of the rank and file, and not a few have unholstered pistols tucked into their waist-belts.

The company colour-bearer has a broad black shoulder-belt to carry the colour-pole, the flag itself being of the First National Flag design, with six white stars arranged around a seventh star in the blue canton. N.C.O.s chevrons are the same colour as the shoulder-straps and trouser-stripes. The company 'band', in addition to the drummer illustrated, consisted of a side-drummer and fifer, the former carrying his drum on a black leather shoulder-belt. Both musicians are wearing not the usual képi, but 'pork-pie' style of fatigue caps like the pattern worn in the U.S. – Mexican War.

1861-65

Private, Alexandria Rifles; Private, Woodis Rifles, Full Dress; Drum Major, 1st Virginia Volunteers, Full Dress

A Confederate militia company raised in Norfolk, Virginia, in 1858, the Woodis Rifles were named after a mayor of the city, Hunter Woodis. Their uniform was one of the most magnificent of the period, consisting of frock-coat of 'hunting-green' with black velvet facings, gilt buttons and much gold lace. The initials of the name, 'W.R.' was repeated on the hat-badge and belt-plate. The company maintained an equally impressive band, which was not surprisingly adopted as the regimental band of the 6th Virginia.

The Alexandria Rifles (6th Battalion Virginia Volunteers) also wore green uniforms, but with the more sombre trimming of black lace. These colours were appropriate for a 'rifle' unit: they were the traditional semi-camouflaged colours of European skirmisher corps.

Each company of the 1st Virginia maintained its own distinctive uniform for a period, until a more mundane service uniform was adopted. Field officers wore dark blue frock-coats and trousers, Virginia State buttons and the 'Hardee' hat. Sergeant-Major Pohlé, Drum Major of the 1st Virginia Volunteers, came from a Richmond militia company known as the Virginia Rifles, having served in a U.S. Navy band before the war. Pohlé's magnificent uniform, which would hardly have been out of place in Napoleonic France, was reserved for full dress only. The 1st Virginia's regimental band consisted of thirteen musicians, plus a Corps of Drums of fourteen boys aged sixteen or over; both were disbanded upon the reorganisation of the regiment a year after its inception.

Privates, Louisiana Tiger Zouaves
Chatham Roberdeau ('Rob') Wheat
led a varied career; son of an
Episcopal minister, he served in the
U.S.-Mexican War at the age of
twenty, after which he settled in
New Orleans as a criminal lawyer.
He raised a unit mostly from Irish
'roughs' in New Orleans, officially
known as Wheat's Special Battalion
or the Louisiana Zouaves, but
glorying in the nickname 'Tigers'.

As Major commanding the
'Tigers', Wheat alone could control
the unruly elements from which the
corps was composed. He led them
at First Bull Run where he was shot
through both lungs; told that the

wound was mortal, he replied 'I
don't feel like dying yet', and
indeed survived to lead his tough
battalion in the Valley campaign.
After his mortal wound at Gaines'
Mill, the 'Tigers' were never again
an effective fighting unit when
deprived of Wheat's leadership
and discipline.

The Louisiana 'Tigers' wore a
typical Zouave costume, consisting
of red stocking-cap with blue tassel,
dark brown jacket with red braid in
varying patterns, red shirts and
sashes, and trousers made from
bed-ticking, sometimes white with
blue stripes or mixtures of red,
white and blue. Also known as the

1st Louisiana Special Battalion, the
'Tigers' included the following
exotically-named companies:
Walker Guards ('A'), Tiger Rifles
('B'), Delta Rangers ('C'), Catahoula
Guerrillas or Old Dominion Guards
('D'), and the Wheat Life Guards
('E'). The battalion formed part of
the 1st Louisiana Brigade, consisting
also of the 6th and 8th Louisiana
Regiments and The Pelican
Regiment (7th Louisiana); the entire
brigade adopted the nickname of
Wheat's corps, calling themselves
the 'Louisiana Tigers'.

1861-65

Private and 1st Lieutenant; 1st Battalion, Louisiana Zouaves

The Louisiana Zouave Battalion was raised from Europeans in New Orleans, and wore a typical Zouave-style costume; the main difference between the uniforms of the officers and men was in the style of jacket, the rank and file having proper 'Zouave' sleeved waistcoats, while the officers had a type of shell-jacket with standing collar, bearing the rank markings on the cuffs and collar. The regiment was nicknamed 'The Pelicans' from the design of the State seal often borne upon the waist-belt. The regiment served throughout the war,

maintaining a fine record.

Several other Louisiana units bore the name 'Pelicans': the Pelican Greys (Company 'A' 2nd Louisiana Infantry), the Pelican Guards (Infantry Company 'B', Louisiana Legion), the Pelican Rangers ('D' and 'H', 3rd Louisiana), and the Pelican Rifles ('A' 2nd Louisiana, 'K' 3rd Louisiana).

4th Texas Volunteers; Sergeant, Company 'B'; Private, Company 'H'; Private, Company 'A'

The 4th Texas Volunteers were organised in October 1861 at 'Camp Texas' near Richmond, Virginia, from the volunteer companies which had arrived from Texas, command of the regiment going to Colonel John Bell Hood, later promoted to General. Including volunteer companies named the Austin City Light Infantry, the Mustang Greys and the Grimes County Greys, the plate illustrates the uniforms of three companies: the Hardeman Rifles ('A'), the Tom Green Rifles ('B'), and the Porter Guards ('H').

The uniform worn by all three consisted of a basic all-grey fatigue style uniform, with certain company distinctions: the Hardeman Rifles wore grey or black 'slouch' hats, the Porter Guards grey képis, and the Tom Green Rifles grey slouch-hats and black braid trimming on the jacket and trousers, N.C.O.s chevrons being of the same black braid.

Black leather equipment was worn by all companies, the 'Lone Star' device being commonly displayed on the belt-plates and sometimes (unofficially) as a hat-badge.

The sergeant illustrated is further distinguished from the other ranks by a crimson waist-sash.

Infantry in 'Butternut', 1865

As the Confederacy declined and the Federal blockade tightened, the Confederate uniform underwent a gradual change in colour from grey to that illustrated in this plate. Once the supply of grey cloth had run out, the material was dyed with 'butternut' (nut-shells and rust being a common concoction) which produced an endless variety of brown, buff and light khaki shades. This dress, often combined with captured Federal items and pieces of civilian clothing, was in a way a rudimentary form of camouflage, and led to the nickname of 'Butternuts' being bestowed upon the Confederate troops by the Federals.

The two 'uniforms' illustrated are taken from contemporary photographs; both men wear battered felt hats and ragged, patched clothing. The fashion of wearing the trousers tucked into the socks was very popular in both armies. The equipment was reduced to a minimum, generally consisting of only haversack, canteen and tin mug, the remainder having been thrown away, lost, or never issued. Cartridge-pouches were rarely used, it being easier to carry the cartridges loose in the pockets. Leather equipment was often issued in 'natural' or brown colouring when the supply of black dye ran out. One of the men illustrated has a captured Federal 'gum blanket', the rubber-muslin 'poncho' being used as a shoulder-roll to contain what would not fit into the haversack. After late 1862 the shortage of shoes in the Confederate army was desperate, leather was scarce or unavailable, so in many cases 'utility' or substitute shoes were being made: those illustrated are of the type made by nailing leather onto a wooden sole, with old horse-shoes fastened underneath as boot-irons.

Captain, Artillery, Full Dress; Gunner, Service Dress

Confederate Artillery uniforms supposedly conformed to the regulation style worn by other branches of the army, with the red distinguishing colour, worn on the képi, facings and trimming. In practice, however, it is possible that few enlisted men ever wore the prescribed frock-coat, a variety of non-regulation styles being worn on active service.

The officer in this plate wears the regulation uniform; on campaign, brimmed felt hats and short jackets were more commonly used. The gunner is shown in a red-piped shell-jacket, which uniform (taken from contemporary information) was just one of a myriad of styles used even within the same company. One gunner of each team also carried a large leather haversack used to convey cartridges from limber or ammunition-waggon to cannon, providing that there was time and opportunity to obey the conventional drill. Another member of the team carried a combined sponge and rammer, which fulfilled the dual rôle of ramming down the charge and swabbing out the cannon-barrel to clear the bore of any fouled, burnt powder.

Private, Rifle Volunteers; Private, Palmetto Guards; Private, Infantry Volunteers

The figures illustrated in this plate (taken from contemporary photographs and engravings) show typical volunteer and militia uniforms worn in the early months of the Civil War by the Confederacy. One uniform is based upon a much earlier style, including a flat-topped forage cap covered with black 'waterproof' as worn during the U.S.-Mexican War, and braided shell-jacket. The rifleman wears a leather 'hunting shirt', a traditionally-American garment worn by 'backwoodsmen' and

pioneers for more than a century prior to the Civil War.

The Palmetto Guards (South Carolina) uniform is based upon a photograph of Edmund Ruffin, a prominent agriculturist and author, and an ardent secessionist. Ruffin (1794–1865) claimed to have fired the first shots at both Fort Sumter and First Bull Run; his claim of having fired the first shot of the war seems a dubious one. The Palmetto Guards appear to have worn a civilian-style suit, with the addition of military equipment and hat. The hat had an upturned brim on the right-hand side, with the letters 'P.G.' and a laurel wreath on the front;

another small badge (probably the state emblem) was worn on the left-hand side. Two companies of South Carolina troops bore the title 'Palmetto Guards': Company 'I' of the 2nd S.C. Infantry, and 'A' of the 18th Battalion, S.C. Siege Artillery. The same name was also used by Company 'C' of the 19th Georgia Infantry.

The rifleman is armed with a custom-built, heavy-barrelled sniper's rifle, with brass telescopic sight running the length of the barrel, and a 'set' trigger.

Commander, U.S. Navy, Summer Campaign Dress, 1862; Captain, U.S. Navy, Undress, 1862

U.S. Navy full dress uniforms for officers included a bicorn hat, worn with the frock-coat; its use, however was as restricted as that of its Army counterpart, the dress illustrated being the most common wear on service.

Rank-markings after 1863 were as follows: Rear-Admiral: eight ¼-inch bands of lace on sleeves, gold star above top band; silver fouled anchor and two stars on shoulder-bars; cap-badge of two silver stars in wreath. Commodore – as Rear-Admiral, but seven laces on sleeve,

silver star and gold fouled anchor on shoulder-bars, silver fouled anchor in cap-wreath. Captain – six sleeve-laces, silver eagle resting on anchor on shoulder-bars; cap-badge as Commodore. Lieutenant-Commander – four sleeve-laces, silver fouled anchor and two gold oak-leaves on shoulder-bars; cap-badge as Commodore. Lieutenant – three sleeve-laces, silver fouled anchor and two gold bars on shoulder-bars; cap-badge as Commodore. Master – two sleeve-laces, shoulder-bars as Lieutenant but one gold bar, cap-badge as Commodore. Ensign – one sleeve-lace, silver fouled anchor on

shoulder-bars; cap-badge as Commodore. Gunner – gold star on sleeve, plain gold lace shoulder-bars, no device within cap-wreath. Boatswain – as gunner, but silver letter 'B' on shoulder-bars. Carpenter – as Gunner, but no badge on sleeve, letter 'C' on shoulder-bars. Sailmaker – as Gunner, but no sleeve-badge. Midshipman – as Gunner, no shoulder-bars. Master's Mate – as Midshipman, but single-breasted coat.

The peaked undress cap was often replaced by the straw hat in summer.

Seaman, Confederate Navy; Petty Officer, U.S. Navy, Summer Dress
Confederate seamen wore grey cloth jackets and trousers or grey woollen 'frocks' with white duck collars and cuffs, black hats and black handkerchiefs; the rating illustrated, however, shows the dress common to both navies in action, allowing both comfort and freedom of movement. Confederate petty officers wore black 'fouled anchor' rank badges on the right or left sleeve depending on rank (as in the Federal Navy) (dark blue badges when white summer dress was worn). In both navies, chief petty officers wore jackets like those of the junior commissioned ranks. Crews of Confederate privateers were officially civilians, only the officers having Confederate commissions; they therefore wore ordinary civilian dress.

The U.S. Petty Officer is shown in white 'summer rig'; the rank-badge was worn on the left-hand sleeve by lower ranks and the right-hand sleeve by Boatswain's Mates and higher. In ordinary dress, the uniform was similar in cut, but in dark blue. The 'sailor collar' of the blouse bore a small star badge in the rear corners. The Petty Officer is shown armed with a heavy-bladed naval cutlass, together with a 'Navy' pistol. Frequently, combinations of 'blues' and 'whites' were worn in the same uniform, usually at the commanding officer's discretion.

Private, 7th U.S. Cavalry, Campaign Dress, 1876
The 1874 grey flannel shirt was often worn without a coat during a summer campaign. The 1872 campaign hat could be worn brim-up with the help of two pairs of hooks and eyes – or down for extra sun protection. This private is loading his 1873 Colt Army revolver, the famous .45-calibre 'Peacemaker' (or 'Thumb-buster' as the soldiers called it).

First Lieutenant William W. Cooke, 7th U.S. Cavalry, Campaign Dress, 1876
Custer and many of his officers campaigned in hardy buckskin coats. Some favoured the issue sky blue trousers, while others preferred buckskin legwear. Cooke, the 7th's adjutant, holds the .45-calibre U.S. Carbine Model 1873, better known as the Springfield carbine. A 'fireman's shirt' is visible beneath his coat.

Sergeant Robert H. Hughes, 7th U.S. Cavalry, Campaign Dress, 1876
In 1874 enlisted men received a new sack coat piped with yellow cord to replace the plaited fatigue blouse introduced in 1872. Hughes carried Custer's personal guidon, which was lost at the Last Stand. These are based on the uniform regulations of the day, contemporary photographs, the testimony of white survivors of the battle, and artifacts on display at the Smithsonian Institution, West Point Museum, Custer Battlefield National Monument, Monroe County Historical Museum and in private collections.

WORLD WAR I

Brigadier General (acting) Douglas MacArthur, Commander U.S. 84th Brigade, 1918
Homeward bound MacArthur wears a typically fantastic garb. His cap is regulation, but the scarf (knitted by his mother) and fur coat were definitely not.

General John J. Pershing, Commander-in-Chief American Expeditionary Force, Boulogne, June 1917
'Black Jack's uniform is the standard officers' version of the 1902 olive drab service dress with bronzed buttons and badges.
   Equipment includes a mounted officer's russet leather garrison belt with pistol magazine pouch.

Colonel Nimon, Officer Commanding 11th Ammunition Train, France, 1918
The overseas cap with black and gold piping was standard for all officers. Note the rank distinction lace on the greatcoat cuffs. The single inverted gold chevron indicated three months or more service since war was declared east of the 37th meridian west of Greenwich.

WORLD WAR I

Private of Infantry, Marching Order, Tours, France, June 1918
On arrival in Europe, the 1902 olive drab uniform began to be modified. The campaign hat was replaced by the steel helmet and 'overseas' cap, and the canvas leggings by puttees. Shortages of uniforms were often made up from British stocks. This is Model 1910 field equipment with either British or U.S. version of the small box respirator and a U.S. Magazine rifle Cal.30, M.1903 with M.1905 bayonet.

Lieutenant, U.S. 305th Machine-gun Battalion, Field Service Order, Watten, 19 May 1918
The steel helmet was almost identical externally to the British pattern. The arm of service emblem appeared on the tunic collar and badges of rank on the shoulder straps. In addition to his American M.1910 web belt and M.1912 holster, he also wears a British Sam Browne belt, and either a British or U.S. version of the small box respirator. His weapon is a U.S. revolver .45 Colt New Service M.1909

Private of Infantry, Marching Order, Tours, France, June 1918
This is the rear view of the same infantryman. The M.1910 'long' pack was a sort of envelope; personal clothing and possessions were rolled inside the blanket and tent half, which were then placed on the open pack, and the sides of the pack were strapped over it. The 'meat can pouch', which actually contained the mess-tin and iron rations, was laced to the top of the pack, and entrenching tool and bayonet were strapped to the sides of the pack.

WORLD WAR I

Private, 16th Infantry Regiment, France, April 1918
This is the uniform in which the American Expeditionary Force landed in France. The cords on the campaign hat indicated arm of service. He carries an M.1910 cartridge belt, water-bottle and a U.S. Magazine rifle Cal.30 M.1903.

Corporal Alvin C. York, 82nd Division, Argonne Forest, 8 October 1918
The American hero, winner of the Congressional Medal of Honor, French *Croix de Guerre*, and many other awards, wears the olive drab overseas cap and pattern of greatcoat for non-mounted enlisted men. Based on a photograph taken at Châtel-Chéréry, the scene of his famous raid; York was later promoted to sergeant.

Private of Infantry, Winter Guard order, 1918
The earflap cap and Mackinaw were made of waterproof cotton duck lined with olive drab cloth. Later patterns had a khaki cloth roll collar. He has the M.1910 cartridge belt and a U.S. Magazine rifle Cal.30 M.1903.

WORLD WAR I

**Trooper of Cavalry, Rennes
Barracks, 30 May 1918**
The uniform was basically identical
to that of dismounted personnel
except that the breeches were
reinforced on the inside of the legs,
and leather gaiters were supposed
to have been worn in place of the
canvas leggings. The equipment is
M.1910 infantry equipment, and
1912 cavalry equipment (horse
furniture). The weapons are a 1903
pattern bayonet, and 1913 pattern
cavalry sabre, which had bronzed
metal fittings, and scabbard
covered in olive drab canvas.

WORLD WAR I

2nd Lieutenant Field E. Kindley, 148th Aero Squadron, France, 9 September 1918
Kindley wears regulation officer's service dress with bronzed badges and wings for Military Aviators which was introduced on 15 August 1917, and the British Sam Browne belt.

Captain 'Eddie' V. Rickenbacker, Commander 94th Aero Squadron, Toul, France, September 1918
Rickenbacker wears a British Royal Flying Corps field service cap, Military Aviator's wings, an unofficial squadron badge (butterfly) and the British Sam Browne belt.

Enlisted Man, United States Air Service, France, 1918
At first American troops did not have a summer uniform, and so it was permitted to remove the tunic and wear the khaki flannel shirt, as shirt-sleeve order.

WORLD WAR I

Private First Class, 2nd U.S. Cavalry, Field Dress, 1918
American cavalrymen went to France in the woollen 1912 service uniform. Special combat gear included a steel trench helmet manufactured along British guidelines and a gas mask, which was housed in a pouch slung over the right shoulder. The 1917-pattern leggings were made of canvas and faced with russet leather.

2nd Lieutenant, 2nd U.S. Cavalry, Service Dress, 1918 (in background)
2nd lieutenants had plain shoulder loops on their service coats, but all other officers were issued metallic

insignia to show their rank there. This subaltern's horse died in the Model 1917 officer's field saddle and Model 1912 combination halter-bridle.

Major George S. Patton, 3rd U.S. Cavalry, Full Dress Uniform, 1929 (at right)
This basic uniform was introduced in 1902, modified in 1907 and 1911, and finally replaced in 1938. The 1921-pattern officer's dress boots are worn with nickel-plated spurs and chains. Among Patton's medals are the Distinguished Service Cross and Distinguished Service Medal, which he won with the Tank Corps

in World War I.

Captain, Machine-Gun Squadron, 1st Cavalry Division, Service Dress, 1924 (at centre)
This officer's working attire consists of the 1921 service hat, the 1924-pattern service shirt and breeches, and pair of undress boots. Note the 1924-pattern squadron insignia on his collar (an MG separated by crossed sabres). The 1921-pattern insignia had an MG surmounting crossed sabres. The captain is tinkering with a jammed Model 1917 Browning .30-calibre heavy water-cooled machine-gun.

Major-General A. M. Patch, Commander U.S. forces, Guadalcanal, 1942–3

Patch wears the basic khaki drill tropical uniform of the U.S. army with his service dress peaked cap. Equipment and weapons consist of a basic webbing belt, leather automatic pistol holster and a U.S. .45 1911 or 1911A1 automatic pistol.

Private 23rd Infantry Division, Guadalcanal, 1942–3

The one-piece olive-drab herringbone-twill overall was originally intended for fatigues, but was found to be the most practical stop-gap combat dress available at the beginning of the war.

He wears the standard woven waist-belt, with ammunition pouches and cotton bandoliers for additional ammunition, and carries a 1903 Springfield.

Sergeant (Grade 4) Armoured Forces, Tunisia, 1943

The composition helmet was intended as a lightweight protection for the head from possible injury inside the tank. The zip-fronted field jacket has the early style of pockets, which were later replaced by vertical slash pockets.

The belt is the basic web with cartridge case and brown leather pistol holster. His weapon is the U.S. .45 1911A1 (Colt 45) automatic pistol.

WORLD WAR II

Private 3rd Infantry Division, Italy, 1943–4
Here the greatcoat is being worn over the field jacket, together with winter trousers and rubber boots. Under the helmet the soldier wears the knitted woollen cap.

The private's weapon is the U.S. .300 in. M1 carbine.

Staff Sergeant (Grade 3) Armoured forces, Solomon Islands, 1943
In the Far East the most common tank outfit was the one-piece herringbone twill overall, with the lightweight fibre helmet and standard woven belt with leather pistol holster. His weapon is a U.S. .45 M.1928 A1 Thompson sub-machine-gun.

Merrill's Marauders, Northern Burma, March 1944
The U.S. answer to Wingate's Chindits was the 530th Composite Unit (Prov.), better known under its more romantic name of Merrill's Marauders. Every soldier found, by a process of elimination, his ideal combat dress.

Here the standard woven belt, with ammunition pouches and water bottle, is worn with the U.S. M.1 carbine, M.4 knife bayonet, and native *kukri*.

WORLD WAR II

Private of Infantry 30th Infantry Division, Normandy, June 1944
Camouflage uniforms were worn by certain units in Normandy but were immediately withdrawn when it was found that personnel wearing them were being mistaken for *Waffen-SS* men.

The equipment is standard U.S. infantry.

Major 82nd Airborne Division, Normandy, June 1944
The standard parachutist's uniform was similar to the M.1943 combat dress but with different pocket arrangement. Helmets were often camouflaged in this way as well as having rank badges painted on the back.

There was also a woven waistbelt, pistol ammunition pouch, water bottle and field glasses.

Private 34th Infantry Division, Italy, 1945

This rear view shows the M.1943 combat dress.

The equipment shown was a direct development of the first fully-integrated infantry equipment issued in 1910. With only minor modifications it remained in use until the mid-1950s. The pack shown is the 1928 model which was made up of short blanket roll, meat pack and entrenching tool. The bayonet could either be worn on the left hip or attached to the left side of the pack. On his left hip he wears the smaller, more compact gas mask, and on the right the water bottle.

The rifle is a U.S. .300 inch M1 (Garand).

Lieutenant-General Patton, Commander 3rd U.S. Army, Normandy, 1944

Patton wears the M.1944 U.S. version of the British battle dress, with his rank badges appearing on the helmet, shirt collar, and shoulder straps. He wears a non-regulation brown leather officer's belt with his silver-plated Colt .45 'Peacemaker' with 4½-inch barrels and ivory grips, and a .357 Smith and Wesson Magnum with blued finish.

Sergeant Major 26th U.S. Cavalry, Class-A Uniform, 1941
For garrison duty at Fort Stotsenburg, the 1926-pattern service coat and breeches, 1912 garrison belt with holstered .45-calibre automatic, and 1931-pattern laced boots were worn. The Department of the Philippines shoulder patch was displayed on the coat. The sun helmet was donned at the discretion of the officer of the day.

Private 26th U.S. Cavalry, Summer Field Dress, 1942
Suntan coloured shirts and breeches served as the regiment's campaign uniform during the withdrawal to, and siege of, Bataan. World War 1-style tin helmets were given a coat of slick-finish green paint and then sprinkled with sand when the paint was still wet. The 26th was armed with the M1 .30-calibre rifle and .45-calibre automatic pistol. Mounts were decked out in the Model 1928 modified McClellan saddle and full packs.

Captain C. Cosby Kerney, 26th U.S. Cavalry, Summer Field Dress, 1942
The 26th's officers were still attired in the 1924-pattern service shirt and breeches. A compass case occupied a spot on the 1921 officer's field belt in front of the holster. Officers and men always secured their pistols to a lanyard draped around the neck. The gas mask case rested on the left hip from a strap slung over the opposite shoulder. Kerney was the only man in the 26th to use the old Model 1903 Springfield rifle in action against the Japanese. This plate based on information and artifacts furnished by Colonel C. Cosby Kerney, U.S. Army (Retired), who served as a captain with the 26th Cavalry in the Luzon and Bataan campaigns.

WORLD WAR II

Private, 2nd Infantry Division, Ardennes 1944
This soldier is wearing the M. 1943 combat dress with the special rubber winter boots and standard U.S. army equipment. His weapon is the U.S. .30 M1 carbine.

Private William C. Mullins, 50th Armoured Infantry Regiment, Germany 1945
Personnel in armoured divisions tended to wear the field jacket over the one-piece overall, as shown here. The basic woven waistbelt has ammunition pouches for the U.S. .30 M1 rifle (Garand semi-auto) which is fitted with the M1 bayonet.

Private of Infantry, Canadian 1st Army, Reichswald Forest, February 1945
The leather jerkin was the World War 1 innovation which enjoyed long life as a popular and comfortable winter garment. This soldier is carrying a German rocket launcher projectile (280mm).

Midshipman 1st Class, U.S. Naval Academy, Annapolis, Summer, 1941
This Brigade Chief Petty Officer wears the special cadet rank badges on the upper right sleeve, and narrow gold lace rings of a midshipman on his cuffs. This uniform is still in current use.

The midshipman is equipped with U.S. .300 Enfield 1917 rifle and M.19 bayonet.

Lieutenant Paul L. Joachim, America, November 1943
This officer wears the regulation greatcoat with rank distinction lace on the shoulder straps and in black on the cuffs. The newly introduced side or 'garrison' cap bore the U.S. Navy badge on the right, and rank badge on the left front.

Captain, America, 1942
The blue service dress was worn by officers, warrant officers and chief petty officers, as well as by officers in the various auxiliary organisations such as the Coast Guard and Maritime Service.

WORLD WAR II

Petty Officer 3rd Class, America, 1941
The rating badge on the right sleeve indicated that the sailor belonged to the seaman branch. The blue 'Donald Duck' hat was not popular because of its association with the Walt Disney character and so the white working hat was worn almost exclusively during the war.

Shore Patrolman, London, England, July 1942
Here the white working hat, which showed up well in the black-out, is being worn with the peacoat, and canvas gaiters which were issued to ratings for wear on duty on land.
Special equipment carried includes night stick, woven belt, and gas mask.

Chief Petty Officer, America, 1941
The cap badge is the special pattern for C.P.O.s and the jacket was similar to that worn by officers, except that it had eight instead of six buttons. C.P.O.s with less than twelve years' service were not entitled to gold chevrons. Each red stripe on the left cuff represented four years' service.

1941-45

Admiral William D. Leahy, Washington, 1943
As President Roosevelt's personal Chief of Staff, Leahy wears a gold lanyard on his light khaki service dress. The wearing of gold chin strap and peak embroidery was optional with all but full dress.

Vice Admiral Halsey, Pearl Harbor, 1942
Halsey wearing white service uniform has just been awarded the Distinguished Service Medal. The white uniform for chief petty officers was open and worn with white shirt and black tie.

Seaman, America, 1943
In summer ratings wore the white undress uniform with hat, which for cadets had a blue line around the top of the turn back. They also wore the standard army pattern woven ammunition belt. Ratings were armed with the U.S. .300 Enfield 1917 rifle and M.1942 bayonet.

WORLD WAR II

Petty Officer 2nd Class, Atlantic Ocean, 1942
Rank badges were often painted in red for ratings and yellow for officers on the front of the anti-blast helmet. Foul weather clothing included the oilskin or 'slicker' suit and waterproof boots or 'arctics'. Petty officers wore a woven waist-belt with a leather pistol holster.

Seaman 2nd Class, Atlantic Ocean, 1943
The rating wears the M.1940 steel helmet with his division painted on the front, winter jacket and dungaree trousers.

Seaman 1st Class, South Pacific, 1945
The water-repellent 'jungle cloth' winter jacket is here worn with kapok life jacket and blue dungaree trousers, and 'arctics'. The helmet is the special 'Talker Mk. II' which was designed to be worn over headphones, by personnel on communications duty.

Lieutenant Junior Grade Andrew Vanderwall, *U.S.S. Princeton*, Saipan, June 1944
Over the AN-S-31 (Army Navy Summer 31) flying suit, this Avenger pilot wears a 'life preserver vest', revolver suspended on the left breast from an ammunition belt, knife, and combat or 'escape' shoes.

Captain W. F. Kline, U.S.N.
Kline wears the green working uniform for naval aviation personnel with black rank distinction lace on the cuffs. He is holding an ashtray given to him by members of the Fleet Air Arm.

Flight Deck Officer, *U.S.S. Princeton*, Saipan, June 1944
Carriermen wore brightly coloured cloth helmets and shirts with their function or team number painted in large letters or numerals on the front and back.

Corporal U.S. Marine Contingent, London, England, October 1942
On the left sleeve of his dress blue tunic he wears corporal's stripes and four year service stripe. The badges on the left breast are the sharpshooters badge and medal with dates of awards, expert rifleman's and pistol shot's bar suspended beneath it. He wears full dress white waist-belt with brass plate and white bayonet sheath, and is armed with the U.S. .30 Calibre M1 rifle (Garand).

Marine Harry Kiriziane in the ruins of Naha, Okinawa, May 1944
From March 1944 the typical Marine camouflage uniform began to be replaced by a new two-piece herringbone-twill (Olive Drab No. 7) combat uniform, with 'U.S.M.C.' and corps badge printed in black on the left breast pocket. The equipment is standard U.S. Army woven type. This marine carries the U.S. .30 Calibre M1 rifle (Garand).

Captain U.S.M.C. Ship Detachment, Augusta, Georgia
The green service dress was basically identical in cut for all ranks, while officers' uniforms were made of gabardine, and other ranks from serge. Ship detachments wore a red shoulder flash in the shape of a rhomboid charged with a yellow sea horse superimposed on a blue anchor, on the left sleeve at shoulder height.

This officer wears the standard army pattern woven belt with pouch for pistol ammunition clips, and brown leather holster. There were two patterns of waist-belt; the belt illustrated had eyelets from which the various items of equipment were suspended, while the belt issued for wear with full equipment did not have the eyelets, since these appeared on the woven ammunition pouches.

Marine, New Britain, February 1943
The fatigue cap with Marine emblem in black on the front is here worn with camouflage jacket, herringbone twill trousers and waterproof boots. The waist-belt is the woven type with ammunition clip pouch and holster. He carries the U.S. .45 M.1928 Thompson A1 sub-machine-gun.

Petty Officer 3rd Class, Samoan Fita Fita Guard
Members of this all-native unit were assigned to guard American Samoa, and wore national dress in the same basic colour schemes as the U.S. Navy. Illustrated here is the white

dress uniform with rating badge on the front of the *Lava-Lava*. Other orders of dress incorporated a khaki drill turban and *Lava Lava*, or red turban and blue *Lava-Lava*. The uniform is completed with the Standard U.S. Army woven belt and ammunition pouches. This man is armed with U.S. .30 Calibre Model 1903 rifle and M.1905 bayonet.

Major Theodor Olsen, Executive Officer 'Lilly Packin Death Falcons' Squadron, 1 Marine Air Wing, Leyte Gulf, October 1944
Olsen wears the AN-S-31 summer flying suit, life jacket and escape shoes. Pilots flying over jungle

regions in the Far East were also equipped with the Type C-1 Emergency Sustenance Vest – an adjustable vest like garment fitted with pockets into which items of survival kit (anything from lavatory paper to fish-sewing kit in plastic container) were conveniently stowed. It was worn under the life jacket and parachute.

Captain Clark Gable, 8th U.S. Army Air Force, England, 1941
Gable wears the typical crushed cap affected by aircrew, and raincoat with rank badges on the shoulder straps.

Lieutenant General Lewis M. Brereton, Commanding General 9th Air Force, England, April 1943
The 'Ike' blouse with diagonal slash pockets was the forerunner of the M.1944 khaki service uniform which became general issue in 1945. On his right breast he wears the Army Distinguished Unit Badge.

Corporal (5th Grade) 9th Air Force, England, April 1943
M.P.s wore army service dress adorned with white cap cover (which sometimes covered the whole cap), white pistol lanyard, gloves, and leggings, and a whistle on a chain on the left breast.

1941-45

Staff Sergeant D. A. Mayo, England, 1944
Mayo wears a two-piece shearling flying suit with type AN (army navy) -H (heated) 16 helmet, A-6 boots and life preserving vest.

1st Lieutenant James G. Stevenson, England, 1943
The A(army) 2 flying jacket was one of the most popular garments and was worn both on and off duty. The beige trousers were known as 'pinks'.

Private Joe Arritola, 9th Air Force, England, 1944
Joe wears the fatigue 'baseball' cap and working overalls on which rank badges were often drawn with indelible pencil.

WORLD WAR II

Navigator, England, 1944
This outfit includes the Type A (army) helmet with A-14 demand oxygen mask, B-15 jacket, A-11 trousers, A-6 boots and A-11 gloves. In his hand he carries a computer.

Gunner, England, 1944
Beginning in 1943 crews of heavy bombers began to be equipped with protective armour against shrapnel, and the first suits were produced by the famous British swordsmiths Wilkinsons, but these were later superseded by the American pattern illustrated. A helmet designed to fit over the earphones was also introduced.

Waist Gunner B-17 bomber, England, 1944
The Type AN-H-16 helmet is here worn with the F-2 electrically heated suit, and special boots. The gunner is armed with a .650 Calibre M-2 machine gun.

Captain, Infantry, Korea, 1953
This helmet cover is an old sandbag and the boots are suede leather. Two types of hand grenade are attached to the flak jacket and the whole figure oozes fatigue.

General Ridgway, Korea, 1952
After a distinguished career in World War II, General Ridgway took over command of the U.S. Eighth Army in the crisis of a withdrawal on 23 December 1950 when the U.N. forces were being pushed south from the Chinese border by half a million Chinese 'volunteers' fighting for the North Koreans. On 11 April 1951, when

General Douglas MacArthur was sacked by President Truman for disagreeing with the 'No attacks across the Yalu River' doctrine, General Ridgway assumed command of all U.N. forces in Korea. On the peak of his fur cap he wears the four stars of his rank over the parachutist's wings.

Infantry Sergeant First Class, Japan, 1953
This man is probably in Japan on 'Rest and Recuperation' from service in The Korean War as evidenced by the 'Butcher's Apron' as the blue and white striped U.N.

medal ribbon for that conflict is known in the British army. Here it is worn at the outer, lower end of the rows of ribbons. On his right chest he wears the U.S. Presidential Unit Citation – at the time America's highest collective award for bravery in the field. His collar badges bear the infantry crossed rifles and the blue badge half hidden under the lapel is the infantry combat badge. The bottle of PX Bourbon concealed behind his back would ensure a warm welcome anywhere in Tokyo.

VIETNAM

Captain, Air Commando
This Air Commando wears a flight suit which he has altered by cutting off the sleeves. His name and pilot's wings are worn on a tape over the left breast. His headgear is the distinctive Air Commando bush hat, always worn with one side turned up. His weapons are an AR15 adopted by the Air Force for the Air Commandos before the Army adopted the M16, and a S & W Model 15 .38 revolver on his left hip in cross draw position.

Dog Handler, Security Police
This SP wears late pattern tiger-striped utilities with a subdued Security Police badge on the left breast pocket. His headgear is the boonie hat used by all sorts of personnel in Vietnam. On his pistol belt he wears the USAF issue pouch for two 20 round M16 magazines, worn upside down so that the magazines will fall into the hand when the flap is opened. On his right hip he carries a S & W Model 15 revolver, spare ammo for which is carried in the two black leather six-round cartridge pouches over his right hipbone. His primary weapon is the CAR15 SMG version of the M16 slung in assault position.

Combat Controller
This CCT wears leaf pattern camo utilities with the dark blue beret of the Combat Control Teams. Silver jump wings are worn as a beret badge. This CCT carries a radio to call in airstrikes and carries multiple canteens. His weapons are the S & W M15, the CAR15, and a Randall fighting knife. Ammo pouches are the same as those worn by the S.P.

Lieutenant, Advisor to the Junk Forces

This officer is well armed with an M16 rifle and a .45 automatic pistol, the latter carried in a commercial rather than a GI issue shoulder holster. Utilities are olive drab with white name and 'U.S. NAVY' tapes. The utility hat is navy blue with rank insignia worn on the front. The equivalent VNN rank insignia is worn on his shirt flap in the centre of his chest.

SEAL

Dressed for operations in the Mekong Delta, this SEAL wears the old style locally produced tiger-striped camouflage utilities. He wears the camo beret often associated with the SEALs and flopped over the left eye in Viet/French fashion rather than in standard U.S. fashion. His weapon is the Ithaca Moden 37 'trench' shotgun. On his pistol belt he wears two CI shotgun shell pouches, each holding 12 extra rounds of 12 gauge buckshot or flechette ammo, two M26 'frags', and a Ka-Bar fighting/survival knife. His boots are standard jungle boots. Face and body camouflage paint is applied in the distinctive pattern associated with the SEALs.

Pilot, Navy Carrier

This naval aviator wears a flight suit (green and orange flight suits were also worn). Over it, he wears a 'g-suit' and survival gear. He carries a strobe, .38 calibre revolver, .38 special ammo bandolier, and jet pilot's survival knife in pouches and, among other items, a first aid kit, sea biscuits, shark repellent, and signal mirror. He wears the tan side cap and carries his helmet with his name and squadron designation painted on. His boots are brown, standard with naval aviation personnel.

VIETNAM

Sergeant, MIKE Force

This sergeant of the MIKE Forces wears the green beret with 5th SFG flash, tiger stripes and jungle boots. Subdued name and 'MIKE FORCE' tapes as well as subdued parachutist's wings and combat Infantryman's badges are worn on his chest. The MIKE Force insignia is also worn on his left breast pocket. His weapon is the .45 automatic pistol.

Colonel 'Bull' Simmons

He wears his green uniform with trousers bloused into black combat boots. The Ranger tab on his right shoulder is that of his World War II unit – the 6th Ranger Bn. The bars on his right sleeve each denote six months' overseas combat duty. Vietnamese parachutist's wings and a Philippine Presidential Unit Citation are visible on his right breast, while U.S. master parachutist's wings and Combat Infantryman's badge along with the many ribbons denoting long and courageous service adorn his left breast.

MACV/SOG Recon Team Member

This figure is dressed for a covert recon mission into Laos, Cambodia, or North Vietnam. A bandanna made from an OD bandage is worn around his head. A canvas duck survival vest with sleeves and collar sewn to it is worn in lieu of a shirt. Clothing is dyed black so he can blend with the shadows. The snap links and leg straps of his STABO rig are clearly visible. Canvas leggings are worn over the jungle boots to help keep the leeches out. Among his many weapons are a Browning Hi-Power 9mm auto in a GI leather shoulder harness, a 'Swedish K' 9mm SMG, a sawed off M79 grenade launcher loaded with anti-personnel rounds, a Randall fighting-survival knife and M26 grenades.

Sergeant, Marine Corps

The dress blues uniform was not commonly worn in Southeast Asia but this sergeant is on embassy guard duty or sea duty aboard a carrier, battleship, or cruiser. His blue tunic with collar, shoulder sleeve stripes, front, and bottom piped in red and three vertical buttons on the cuffs is the standard dress item for enlisted Marines. The gold chevrons on scarlet are worn to denote rank. The single chevron on the sleeve denotes four years' service. The light blue trousers with scarlet stripes are standard with this uniform. White service hat, belt, and gloves round out the uniform to give the appearance which makes Marine honour guards so impressive. His weapon is the M14 rifle.

Marine Major General Lewis Walt

Major General (later Lieutenant General) Walt was probably the most widely recognized Marine general officer in Vietnam, and like most USMC generals, still looks like a fighting infantryman. He wears green herringbone utility uniform with stars on the collar to denote his rank. He also wears the standard steel helmet with camouflage cover. On his pistol belt are a 1911 .45 auto and double magazine pouch. Typical of Marine Corps general officers, Gen. Walt wears only standard issue equipment.

Marine Infantryman ('Grunt'), Circa 1965

This Marine infantryman wears utilities with fatigue cap, which has the Marine Corps emblem stenciled on the front. The M14 rifle is carried with spare magazine pouches worn on the belt.

Tunnel Rat

This 'tunnel rat' has removed his gas mask, though if the tunnel were still filled with CS gas it would be worn. Because of the heat and closeness in the tunnels, he wears only his trousers and jungle boots. A piece of OD towel or bandage is used as a sweatband. Only the 1911 .45 auto and angle-headed flashlight will be carried, though many tunnel rats also carried some type of radio; a miner's torch was sometimes used in lieu of the flashlight. His dog tag chain is worn inside of plastic tubing to prevent it turning green and from irritating his neck. A P38 can opener is also worn on the chain.

Helicopter Pilot

This pilot wears green utilities rather than the NOMEX flight suit, and black combat boots instead of jungle boots. Many aviators preferred the standard boot. His rank and branch insignia are subdued as is his First Aviation Brigade shoulder sleeve insignia. His locally made assault helicopter company pocket patch, however, is brightly coloured. His mesh survival vest is half off, but the holster for his .38 Special revolver and some of the pouches containing survival radio, first aid kit, etc., are still visible. He carries the light aviation helmet in his right hand.

Grenadier, 9th Infantry Division

This 'grunt' has been slogging through the Mekong Delta. Tucked into the rubber band around his camo helmet cover are cigarettes and matches in a plastic case and jerky wrapped in foil. His vest is designed especially for grenadiers to allow the weight of extra 40mm grenades to be evenly distributed. The butt and muzzle of his M79 grenade launcher are visible in his right hand. He wears the subdued 'cookie' 9th Division insignia on his left shoulder.

1960-84

Captain, 10th Special Forces Group

On his beret the officer illustrated wears the flash of the 10th Special Forces Group. The oval backing of his senior parachutist's badge also identifies him as a member of the 10th SFG.

The bars designating this officer's rank are worn on his beret flash. The Combat Infantryman's badge and ribbons on his left breast and the Republic of Vietnam Jump Wings and U.S. Presidential Unit Citation on his right breast identify a Vietnam veteran. Also on his right breast is the oak leaves and acorn badge identifying him as an 'Einzelkaempfer', a graduate of the

West German Ranger programme.

The arrow patch of the Special Forces is worn at the shoulder along with the light blue airborne tab.

Sergeant, Special Forces, 'Project Delta' – Vietnam

This sergeant wears one of the camouflage patterns sometimes incorrectly called 'Tiger Stripes'. This four colour (two greens, a brown, and a black) pattern came into use during 1968. Around his head this trooper wears a green bandanna, probably an olive drab bandage or piece of a towel. His load bearing harness is the STABO rig. He wears standard jungle boots

but without the canvas leggings sometimes worn by MACV/SOG troopers.

The pistol is a silenced High Standard .22 automatic. Over his shoulder is slung the CAR-15 (XM177E2) short version of the M.16.

Special Forces Master Sergeant, Vietnam

U.S. Army khaki uniform with Special Forces arrowhead patch and black airborne tab. The flash on his green beret is of the 5th Special Forces Group. The oval behind his parachutist's wings bears the colours of the 5th S.F.G. Trousers are bloused into his combat boots.

SPECIAL FORCES

Airborne Ranger, 1960

The Ranger illustrated wears standard fatigue cap and heavy winter fatigues with the collar turned up to protect his neck while using a rope when climbing or when parachuting. His 'greenies' are tied close to his body so they do not get in his way while climbing or moving silently through the bush. Around his waist he carries a climbing rope.

His weapon is the M.14 7.62mm NATO rifle which was the standard U.S. service weapon between 1957 and 1964.

Sergeant, Special Forces, Operational Group – Delta

Operational Group – Delta is the U.S. counterterrorist unit which is stationed at Fort Bragg, North Carolina. This trooper is dressed for a field operation and wears camouflage utilities and bush hat. His weapon is the M.60 GPMG. This sergeant has added Pachmayr rubber grips to improve the 'feel' of his Colt .45 automatic pistol.

LRRP (Long Range Reconnaissance Patrol) – Vietnam

The LRRP illustrated wears camouflage utilities along with matching bush hat. Around his neck is an OD towel. His standard load bearing rig is the M.56 H-harness/pistol belt combination with lightweight rucksack. The LRRP was normally festooned with canteens. Ready for instant use he carries M.26A1 grenades taped to the ammo pouches at his waist. Smoke grenades such as the one on his left breast, claymore mines, M.34 'Willie Pete' grenades, explosives and demolition cord were also normally carried.

SPECIAL FORCES

Air Force Combat Security Policeman – Vietnam

This Combat Security Policeman wears camouflage to allow him to blend into the scrub and elephant grass which surrounded most air bases. When not out on a sweep or an ambush, he would be likely to wear the dark blue beret originally awarded to the first Combat Security Police graduates of the 'Safeside' Program. In addition to his S & W Model 15 .38 Special revolver he carries the Remington 870 slide action 12 gauge riot gun.

Private First Class, 82nd Airborne

This paratrooper wears the experimental desert camouflage pattern which is appropriate to the 82nd Airborne's possible role in the Rapid Deployment Force. He also wears the maroon beret which was reinstated in the 82nd at the end of 1980. Beret flash and/or crest will vary among sub units of the Division. Jungle boots are worn in preference to the normal black jump boots because of their suitability in hot climates.

The subdued divisional patch of the 82nd 'All American' Airborne and subdued airborne tab are worn. Subdued rank insignia are worn on the collar. His weapon is the standard M.16. This paratrooper would use the MCI-1B steerable parachute for a combat jump.

Sergeant, Air Force Pararescue

The USAF Pararescue Service is one of the world's least known elite forces. Four points of attire set this pararescueman apart. Most noticeable is his maroon beret with the Pararescue badge bearing the motto 'That Others Might Live'. The jump wings on his left breast and the bloused trousers with combat boots identify him as a paratrooper, while the aircrewman's wings above the parachutist's wings designate that he is on flight status. His four stripes identify him as a staff sergeant.

Navy SEAL, Vietnam

This Vietnam era SEAL (Sea Air Land) has probably just landed from a small boat in the Mekong Delta region and is equipped to set an ambush along the Viet Cong trail network through this swampy area. He wears 'Tiger Stripes' camouflage clothing and face paint. His weapon is the Stoner M.63A1 Light Machine-Gun favoured by the SEALs. The 5.6mm Stoner was light (12.5lbs unloaded) and with the 150 round drum magazine illustrated gave the SEALs a lot of firepower. Additional ammunition is carried in belts around the figure's torso.

Navy SEAL

This U.S. Navy SEAL is equipped for a beach incursion, possibly to survey enemy defenses. His inflatable life vest and diving mask are the standard issue items for both the SEALs and UDTs. Since he wears only the wetsuit top with trunks on the bottom he is probably not operating in Northern waters. His weapon is the U.S. Navy Mark 22, Model 0 silenced 9mm pistol manufactured by Smith & Wesson for the SEALs. This weapon is fabricated of stainless steel so it will not rust in salt water.

Navy UDT 'Frogman'

The U.S. Navy UDT (Underwater Demolition Team) wears 'Twin-80s', double 80 cubic feet capacity aluminium tanks which allow him to stay underwater long enough to complete his mission.

This UDT wears a full wetsuit and carries his flippers. In his hand is the U.S. Navy Underwater Knife used by both the UDTs and SEALs. All metal parts of this knife are made of rust resistant non-ferrous metals. It can be carried on the arm as this frogman carries his, on the leg, or at the belt. One edge of the blade has saw teeth, while the other is a normal cutting edge.

SPECIAL FORCES

First Lieutenant, Marine Corps

This Lieutenant wears the distinctive Marine Corps blues. This is the same basic uniform worn by embassy guards and Marine guards aboard cruisers and aircraft carriers. This is the normal USMC dress uniform, though a number one or 'Mess' dress exists for formal wear. The cap badge and collar insignia are the eagle, globe, and anchor. The Sam Browne belt and shoes are highly polished. Not having served during the Vietnam War, this officer has only peacetime ribbons such as the National Defense Service Medal and Good Conduct Medal.

Drill Instructor, Marine Corps

The drill instructor is the real backbone of the Corps, and his campaign hat, blood curdling stare, and clenched teeth growl all identify him as the man who turns civilian 'maggots' into Marines in 11 weeks of boot camp.

This staff sergeant's short sleeve uniform shirt is especially well-suited to the heat and humidity at the two USMC recruit depots – San Diego, California and Parris Island, South Carolina. In true DI fashion, this figure manages to look cool and 'squared away' even after hours of drill.

Lance Corporal, Marine Corps

This lance corporal wears the new camouflage adopted by the corps and carries the M.16 rifle. On his webbed belt he wears the USMC 'Ka-Bar' fighting/utility Bowie style knife. As a Marine infantryman assigned to the Fleet Marine Force, he could be slated to serve in the Rapid Deployment Force. In the Marine Corps, there are two corporal's ranks. One chevron over crossed rifles as worn by this Marine denotes a lance corporal, while two chevrons over the rifles indicates full corporal's rank.

SPECIAL FORCES

Sergeant, Princess Patricia's Canadian Light Infantry, 1975
The Canadian Brigade in Germany is now deployed in the South of Germany with the American army. National identity is shown by the flag on both sleeves, ranks are as in the British army for soldiers but a new system of navy-style gold bars was introduced for officers at the time of the unification of Canada's defence forces in 1968. On the shoulder strap is worn the regimental title (here PPCLI) in light buff woven letters.

General Alexander Haig, Supreme Commander Allied Powers in Europe, 1975
In October 1975 the Federal German Army held a Corps exercise called 'Grosse Rochade' up against the Czechoslovakian border and General Haig, while visiting a German Fallschirmjäger battalion was presented with one of their maroon berets with its plunging eagle badge which he wore for the rest of his visit. As an old infantryman he wears the infantry combat badge on the left breast.

Recon, U.S. Marine Corps
The Recon illustrated wears the same type of flotation vest used by the Navy's UDTs and SEALs. Prepared for a night mission, his face is covered with grease paint camouflage which also makes an effective sun screen during the day. Quite often a rope is carried to allow the four men of the squad to keep contact while swimming under water. This Recon's weapon is the M.16 with M.203 40mm grenade launcher attached. Standard knife for the Recons is the USMC Ka-Bar, but many prefer to carry a Randall or Gerber.

INDEX

Afrique, Corps d' 67
Aide-de-camp 14, 36
Air Commando 116
Air Force 112-4
Airborne Division
  82nd 101
  U.S. Army 123
Airborne Rangers 122
Alabama, 20th Regiment 77
Alarm Companies 9
Alexandria Rifles 83
American Expeditionary Force 93
American Rangers 8
Ammunition Train, 11th 93
Annapolis, Naval Academy 105
Armoured Forces
  Solomon Islands 100
  Tunisia 99
Armoured Infantry Regiment 102
Artillery, 2nd 68

Brigadier-General 14, 42, 93
British Legion 40
British Regiment, 8th 44
Butler's Rangers 29

Canada
  1st Army 104
  2nd Regiment 17
  Infantry 104
  Princess Patricia's Light Infantry 126
Cannoniers-bombadiers 8
Cavalry
  1st U.S. 56, 57
  4th U.S. 57
  5th U.S. 57
  7th U.S. 92
  Confederate Army 71, 72-3
  U.S. Army 49, 50, 52-3, 96, 98, 103
Cavalry-General 56
Charleston Light Dragoons 74
Coloured Infantry, 56th 67
Combat Security Police 123
Commander-in-Chief 14
Compagnies Franches de la Marine 7
Confederate Army 70
  Artillery 88
  General 70
  Infantry 9, 77, 78, 80, 87
  Infantry Volunteers 89
  Rifle Volunteers 89
Confederate Navy 91
Congress's Own Regiment 17
Connecticut 4th Regiment 10
Continental Army 37
Continental Artillery 38
Continental Light Dragoons 24
  1st 23, 41
  1st, Lee's 5th Troop 24
  2nd 39, 41
  3rd 23
  4th 39
Continental Marines, 1776 35
Continental Navy 34
Continental Regiments 15-16
  Additional, Col. Samuel B. Webb's 22
  Additional, Col. Spencer's 22
  Additional (Col. Hartley's) 21
  Additional (Col. Henley's) 21
  Additional (Col. W.R. Lee's) 21
  Artillery Artificers 32
  Unknown officer, 1778 31
Corps d'Afrique 67

De Lancey's Brigade 44
Delaware
  Haslet's regiment 18
Dragoons 46

Ellsworth Zouave Cadets 65
Engineer Corps 38, 70

Foot Regiments, See Continental
  Regiments
French Colonial Artillery 8

General 56, 70, 93, 126
Green Mountain Boys 11

Haslet's Regiment 18
Hazen's Regiment 17
Heavy Artillery 67
Heer's Provost Corps 42
His Majesty's Independent Companies
  of American Rangers 8

Illinois 19th Volunteers 65
Infantry 42, 58
  Canada 104, 126
  Confederate Army 9, 77, 78, 80-1, 89
  U.S. Army 94, 95, 99, 100, 101, 102,
    115, 120
  Volunteers 89
Invalid Corps 69
Irish Brigade 60
Iron Brigade 59
Iroquois 33

Kentucky 1st Cavalry Brigade 75
King's Regiment 44
Knox's Artillery Regiment 13

Lamb's New York Artillery Company
  13, 14
Lieutenant-General 101
Light Artillery 68
Light Company, 2nd Canadian
  Regiment 17
'Lilly Packin Death Falcons' 111
Long Range Reconnaissance Patrol 122
Loyalist officer 29

Machine-gun Battalion 94
Machine-gun Squadron 98
MACV/SOG Recon Team 118
Maine 20th Infantry 59
Major-General 47, 99, 119
Marines 35, 110-1, 119
Maryland
  1st Regiment 27
  2nd Regiment 27
  4th Independent State Troops 12
  6th Regiment 27
  State Marines 35
  Smallwood's Regiment 18
Massachusetts
  3rd Regiment 26
  6th Continental Regiment 15
  8th Regiment 26
  12th Continental Regiment 15
  14th Continental Regiment 16
  14th Regiment 26
  Col. Patterson's battalion 12
  Light Infantry Company 45
Merrill's Marauders 100
Michigan 21st Regiment 60
MIKE Force 118
Militiamen 7, 10

Minutemen 9
Morgan's Rifle Corps 32
Mounted Ranger Battalion 46

New Hampshire 37
  2nd Regiment 28
  2nd Regiment (Col. Enoch Poor's) 16
  2nd Volunteers 64
  4th Regiment 69
  Provincial Regiment 8
New Jersey 37
  3rd Regiment 28
New York 37
  2nd Regiment 17, 18
  3rd Regiment 17
  3rd Regiment of 1776 19
  5th Regiment 28
  5th Zouaves 61
  7th National Guard 63
  14th Volunteers 65
  22nd Regiment 69
  79th Volunteers 62
  Captain Lamb's Artillery 13
  Light Infantry Company 45
  Militia 63
North Carolina
  3rd Regiment 43
  Volunteers 44

Ohio Volunteer Light Artillery 68
Operational Group-Delta 122

Palmetto Guards 89
Pararescue Service 123
Patterson's battalion 12
Pennsylvania
  1st Battalion 19
  3rd Battalion 19
  3rd Cavalry 55
  4th Cavalry 55
  5th Regiment 30
  6th Cavalry 54
  7th Regiment 20
  9th Regiment 20
  11th Regiment 30
  Rifle Regiment 11
  State Marines 35
  State Regiment 30
Philadelphia
  1st Battalion Associators 25
  Light Horse Troop 24
Princess Patricia's Canadian Light
  Infantry 126
Provincial soldiers 9
Pulaski's Legion Infantry 42

Quebec Militia 7
Queen's Rangers 40

Recon 126
Red Jacket 33
Rhode Island
  1st Cavalry 50
  1st Regiment 11
  1st Volunteers 64
  Light Infantry Company 45
  Train of Artillery 13
Rifle Volunteers 89
Rogers' Rangers 8
Royal Highland Emigrants 29
Rush's Lancers 54

Samoan Fita Guard 111
Sea, Air, Land (SEAL) 117, 124

Security Police 116
Sharpshooter Regiments 66
Smallwood's Regiment 18
South Carolina
  1st Regiment 43
  2nd Regiment 43
  Palmetto Guards 89
  Volunteers 81
Special Forces, U.S. Army 122-6
Staff officers 93
  Aide-de-camp 14, 36
  Brigadier-General 14, 36, 42, 48, 70
  Commander-in-Chief 14
  General 56, 70, 115, 126
  General of Cavalry 71
  Lieutenant-General Patton 102
  Major-General 47, 99, 119
Sumter Light Guard 82

Texas
  1st Cavalry 74
  4th Volunteers 86
  8th Cavalry 76
  26th Cavalry 75
  Infantry 81

Underwater Demolition Team 124

U.S. Air Force 112-4, 116
  Air Commando 116
  Combat Security Police 123
  Pararescue Service 123
  Security Police 116
U.S. Air Service 97
U.S. Army
  1st Aviation Brigade 120
  2nd Cavalry 98
  3rd 101
  3rd Cavalry 98
  3rd Infantry Division 100
  9th Infantry Division 120
  10th Special Forces Group 121
  16th Infantry Regiment 95
  23rd Infantry Division 99
  30th Infantry Division 101
  34th Infantry Division 102
  82nd Airborne 123
  82nd Airborne Division 101
  82nd Division 95
  84th Brigade 93
  94th Aero Squadron 97
  148th Aero Squadron 97
  530th Composite Unit (Prov) 100
  Airborne Rangers 122
  Armoured Forces 99, 100
  Cavalry 96, 98

Infantry 94, 95, 115
  Machine-Gun Squadron 98
  MACV/SOG Recon Team 118
  MIKE Force 118
  Special Forces 117, 122-6
U.S. Cavalry 103
U.S. Marines 110, 119, 125, 126
  1st Air Wing 111
U.S. Militiamen 10
U.S. Navy 1, 90, 105, 106-9, 117
  Aviation Personnel 117
  Sea, Air, Land (SEAL) 124
  Underwater Demolition Team 124

Vermont 9th Cavalry 56
Virginia
  1st Cavalry 73
  1st Volunteers 83
  5th Regiment, 1777 31
  6th Regiment of 1777 20
  13th Regiment 25
  Corps of Light Horse 41
  Militia 7

Warner, Co. Seth's Battalion 11
Whitcomb's Rangers 15
Wisconsin, 8th Regiment 60
Woodis Rifles 83

This volume is based upon the illustrations of Malcolm McGregor, Michael Chappel, Pierre Turner, Ernest Lisle Reedstrom and Ken McSwan, first published by Blandford Press in *Uniforms Of The Seven Years War* and *Uniforms Of The American Revolution* by John Mollo, *Uniforms Of The American Civil War* by Philip Haythornthwaite, *Army Uniforms Of World War I*, *Army Uniforms Of World War II*, and *Naval, Air Force and Marine Uniforms of World War II* by Andrew Mollo, *Army Uniforms Since 1945* by Digby Smith, *The United States Cavalry* by Gregory Urwin, *Uniforms Of The Elite Forces* and *Uniforms Of The Indo-China And Vietnam Wars* by Leroy Thompson.

The publishers wish to thank Michael Bowers Editions for help in preparation of this book.